— ≈ —

Quiet Moments for
Working Women

— ≈ —

Quiet Moments for Working Women

Mary Whelchel

SERVANT PUBLICATIONS
ANN ARBOR, MICHIGAN

Vine Books is an imprint of Servant Publications especially designed to serve
evangelical Christians.

Published by Servant Publications
P.O. Box 8617
Ann Arbor, Michigan 48107

Cover design: PAZ Design Group, Salem, OR
Cover photograph: © Steve Chen / Corbis-Westlight

        01 02 10 9 8 7 6

Printed in the United States of America
ISBN 1-56955-078-6

LIBRARY OF CONGRESS CATALOGING-IN-PUBLICATION DATA

Whelchel, Mary.
Quiet moments for working women / Mary Whelchel.
    p.   cm.
ISBN 1-56955-078-6 (alk. paper)
1. Christian women—Prayer-books and devotions—English.   2. Working—
Prayer-books and devotions—English.   I. Title.
BV4844.W54   1999
242'.643—dc21   98-40819
                                                       CIP

Dedication

I lovingly dedicate this book to my dear friend, Lucille Rinaldo, who is now praising the Lord in heaven and continuing to bask in his love. Terminal cancer took her away from us far too soon, but she has impacted my life more than she ever knew. Thank you, Lucille, for demonstrating to all who knew you how to face death with victory and even anticipation. We'll see you soon.

— ∼ —
Acknowledgement
— ∼ —

I am deeply indebted to my staff at *The Christian Working Woman,* who lighten my load and make it possible for me to have time to write books! They are my partners in ministry, and I am blessed to call them friends and co-workers. Thank you, Julie, Karen, Bobbi, Robin, and Michael. You're the best!

ONE

— ∿ —

Don't Throw Away Your Pearls

Do not give dogs what is sacred; do not throw your pearls to pigs. If you do, they may trample them under their feet, and then turn and tear you to pieces.

MATTHEW 7:6

I always had a difficult time understanding this passage. It seemed rather crude, frankly, and I just was not sure what Jesus meant by it. Was he calling people dogs and pigs? That didn't seem right to me.

Then a former working buddy called and suggested that we get together for dinner. God had gotten hold of my life since the last time we had talked, and so I thought, "Great, I'll have dinner with him and share my testimony. Maybe I can help him find Christ as his Savior."

My motives were good, but it didn't work out. All through the evening I kept trying to force a conversation about the Lord, but my friend was more interested in other topics. He wanted to talk about anything *but* spiritual matters. Afterward I felt like a failure; I had wasted a valuable night, I thought.

That's when God reminded me of this passage. Despite my good intentions, I had thrown what was sacred before someone who had no regard for its value. Just as a pig cannot naturally distinguish between pearls and slop, my friend would not be able to receive my sacred "pearls" until his blinders had come off and he had a desire to know more about God.

We need to be discerning about sharing our faith. Do not force your "pearls" at work where they are not wanted or appreciated. Instead, pray for natural openings, and trust God to orchestrate those opportunities for you. Be willing. Be ready. But above all, be wise.

Today's Challenge

To look for a genuine opportunity to share my faith without forcing it on someone who is not ready.

Today's Prayer

Lord, I ask for holy discernment today. Please give me the courage to share my faith, and make me sensitive to those times when it would not be appropriate. Help me to avoid casting my sacred pearl of life in Christ before someone who is not ready to receive it.

TWO

— ❧ —

Work for Jesus

Serve wholeheartedly, as if you were serving the Lord, not men, because you know that the Lord will reward everyone for whatever good he does, whether he is slave or free.

EPHESIANS 6:7

Have you ever been "passed over" for a promotion or raise that you *knew* you deserved? It can be discouraging not to get credit for our contributions at work. And yet, these things happen all the time.

We live and work in a world that is neither fair nor kind. That's because the world is full of people who have a sin problem—including us! And that sin problem creates injustice of all sorts.

Injustice is one of my toughest hurdles. I always want to fight when I think my or someone else's rights are being violated. As you can imagine, this tendency has gotten me into some hot water in my work life. I have to remind myself continually that *if* I serve wholeheartedly as unto the Lord, the recognition and rewards will come in due time.

As Christians, we pick up our paychecks at our place of work, but our real job is pleasing the Lord and working for *him*. Our reward is waiting for us in heaven—but we can reap the benefits now, too. Just imagine how your stress level will drop as thoughts of vengeance and discontent are replaced with calm satisfaction over a job well done!

Today's Challenge

To remember all day long that I report to Jesus, and he will reward his "good and faithful servants."

Today's Prayer

Lord, regardless of what happens today, I want to stay focused on the rewards you have for me for doing good work. Please give me the self-control that I need to handle injustice and unfairness in my workplace without becoming bitter or angry.

THREE

— ~ —

Encouraging Words

Therefore encourage one another and build each other up, just as in fact you are doing.

1 THESSALONIANS 5:11

If you would like to improve your skills at encouraging others, here are some suggestions.

Watch carefully your choice of words. Careless words can be very discouraging. I was once talking with a man who had been very sick for a long time, but was doing much better. However, after this long sickness he was very thin, and the effects of his illness were still showing. I was telling him how happy I was he was doing so well when another person walked up and said, "My, you've aged a great deal."

I'm sure that other person didn't mean to discourage him, but I could see the disheartened look on his face when he heard her observation. It was not an encouraging word.

I often remind myself that I don't have to say everything I think! If the words won't refresh others, I can either keep my mouth shut or change the words. Colossians 4:6 says, "Let your conversation be always full of grace, seasoned with salt, so that you may know how to answer everyone." If you and I will pray for that verse to characterize our lives and practice it by God's power, we will become better encouragers.

We can also encourage ourselves by being cautious about our self-talk. Many of us make our lives much tougher by saying all the wrong things to ourselves. Talk to yourself about who you are in Christ, about how much he loves you, about all his blessings in your life. Tell yourself you can do all things through Christ who strengthens you. Don't babble a bunch of negative junk into your head all day. It will just discourage you, and you need to be your own encourager.

Today's Challenge

To speak words that encourage, not words that discourage. To choose my words carefully and look for opportunities to speak those carefully chosen words of encouragement.

Today's Prayer

Lord, help me to speak words full of grace today, words that will build up others and encourage them. Remind me of how important it is to become an encouraging woman.

FOUR

— ∾ —

Time Wasters

Make the best use of your time, despite all the difficulties of these days.

EPHESIANS 5:16, PHILLIPS

Think about some of your common time wasters. My guess is that interruptions would be near the top of that list. If phones didn't ring, people didn't ask questions, or unexpected meetings weren't called, we could get more done. But let's be realistic: these interruptions are never going to be eliminated entirely. They're part of the job.

Since we can't stop the interruptions, what *can* we do to "work smarter"? Remember: time is a gift from God, a resource provided to each of us in the same, daily measures. While some interruptions are unavoidable and even necessary, we can do some proactive things to minimize our interruptions.

Group your activities, for example. Return and place phone calls at certain times, all together. Go to the copier and the fax machine once or twice a day instead of ten times a day. Interrupt yourself for coffee or refreshments at specified times to help you stay on task longer.

A good time manager has a daily plan for activities and priorities, written down and followed. It can be in an informal format, like a calendar or a pad of paper, or a structured plan like a Day-Timer, but if you consistently use a daily activity plan, you will use your time much more effectively.

Remember, despite all the difficulties you're going to face today, make the best use of your time, because once you spend time, you can never replace it.

Today's Challenge

To be aware of my "time wasters" today, so I can work more effectively and be a better steward of my time.

Today's Prayer

Lord, I need help in managing my time. I know that you expect me to make good use of my time and that I will be accountable to you for how I've spent my twenty-four hours today. So please help me to become a better manager of this wonderful resource.

— ∿ —

Encourage a Hurting Heart

Pleasant words are a honeycomb, sweet to the soul and healing to the bones.

PROVERBS 16:24

Do you know someone on your job who's hurting today? There are always plenty of hurting people around. Some are victims of their own self-inflicted wounds; others suffer because of the poor choices of other people, or due to other circumstances beyond their control.

Hurting people are very receptive to help and friendship. If someone has been distant in the past, reaching out during a time of need may enable you to start building a relationship with that person. A hurting heart can be a tender heart.

Think of someone in your workplace right now who is hurting, and find a way to help him or her. Don't do it just to "win" an opportunity to share your testimony (remember the pearls). Do it because you want to touch that person with the love of Jesus in a practical way. What words of healing could you give that person today?

Maybe you could simply express your concern and tell this person that you are praying for him or her, or send a card. Or perhaps you should do something more. Take that person to lunch. Bring food to his or her home. Offer to baby-sit. The list is endless, but simple actions of love are appreciated when hurt runs deep.

Remember, you have the power through pleasant words and kind actions to bring healing to a hurting person. Don't miss your opportunity today.

Today's Challenge

To be sensitive to the hurting people around me and reach out with words of healing.

Today's Prayer

Lord, sometimes I'm so wrapped up in my own world and my own pain that I forget there are many others around me with hurts of their own, some much worse than mine. Please help me today to be aware of those hurting people you bring across my path, and give me insight to know the words to help them heal.

SIX

— ∾ —

"Harsh" Bosses

Submit yourselves to your masters with all respect, not only to
those who are good and considerate, but also to those who are
harsh.

1 PETER 2:18

Have you ever wanted to send your boss to management
school? In many areas of business there are few educational or
experience requirements for managers. Perhaps you have discovered that your manager's people skills are minimal ... or
nonexistent!

"Submit," Peter challenges us. Submitting to good managers isn't difficult to do. Submitting to someone who falls
short of your managerial expectations definitely goes against
the grain. And yet we are called to submit even to those bosses
who are "harsh," or who are less than "good and considerate."

If you're like me, "submit" is not your favorite word, and
certainly not your favorite command. Submission means humbling yourself, keeping your mouth shut when you'd like to
strike out, refusing to join in a verbal assassination, accepting
instructions and directions without complaining, acknowledging the authority of the position your manager holds.

Submitting with all respect is good spiritual exercise for our
souls. Peter goes on to tell us that it is commendable to God
when we submit to our harsh bosses.

Ah, there's our motivation: it pleases God. While submitting may not be my personal choice, knowing it pleases God helps motivate me.

Today's Challenge

To respect the person to whom I report, regardless of his or her managerial skills, because I want to please God.

Today's Prayer

Lord, help me to see my boss as you do, and teach me how to appropriately submit to this one whom you have placed over me.

— ❧ —

Be a Peacemaker

Blessed are the peacemakers, for they will be called sons of God.
MATTHEW 5:9

Parents know that making peace between children is a part of their job description. From their earliest days, children manage to disrupt the peace by getting into arguments, causing discord, and aggravating each other. At these times we find ourselves in the role of peacemaker.

There are times in every work situation when a peacemaker is needed. Are there feuds going on at your job right now? Do your co-workers refuse to speak to one another? What can you do to make peace? Pray about it, and you just might think of something that could help.

Proverbs 17:9 says, "He who covers an offense promotes love, but whoever repeats the matter separates close friends." One way we can act as peacemakers is not to spread the bad things we hear or see. Cover up the offense; don't gossip about someone's mistake or bad behavior.

Proverbs 15:1 tells us that "a gentle answer turns away wrath, but a harsh word stirs up anger." A peacemaker is a person with gentle words. When someone tells you how angry they are at someone else, find those gentle words to turn away their wrath. If you throw in a few harsh words of your own, you will only add to the conflict.

We need peacemakers in our world of strife—people who

work at bringing peace when conflicts arise in our daily lives. Ask God to give you that skill, that kind of servant heart, so that you are the peacemaker in your world.

Today's Challenge

To be a peacemaker in my home, my workplace, my church, and my family.

Today's Prayer

Lord, please give me the skills and the servant heart that I need to be a real peacemaker.

EIGHT

— ❧ —

Dressing to Glorify God

I also want women to dress ... with decency and propriety, not with braided hair or gold or pearls or expensive clothes, but with good deeds, appropriate for women who profess to worship God.

1 TIMOTHY 2:9

When we feel confident about the way we look, we are less self-conscious. I've found that if I leave the house in the morning feeling that my hair, my outfit, and my overall appearance are close to optimal, then I can forget myself and how I look for the rest of the day. On the other hand, if I'm worrying that my dress is not proper or my hair is not becoming, then all day long I'm thinking about myself, running into the ladies' room to try to improve my appearance, fussing with my clothes—in other words, I'm self-absorbed.

As Christians in the working world, we must not ignore the fact that clothes contribute to others' impressions of us. Our appearance should reflect good taste as well as a sense of personal style. We carry the reputation of Jesus Christ with us, and it's important that our personal appearance never hinders our witness.

We must also be very certain that our appearance does not call undue attention to ourselves. Clothes that are "in style" are not appropriate if they draw more attention to us than to the One who lives in us. So, before we seek the latest fashion, or the current hemline, we need to first be sure that our style of dress reflects our status as women of God.

Today's Challenge

To be certain that how I dress reflects favorably on Jesus, and that I have a sense of modesty pleasing to him.

Today's Prayer

Lord, sometimes I can get swept up in the world's fashion standards. Help me to dress so that my appearance is pleasing to you ... and makes a good impression on my job.

NINE

— ⁓ —

Boring Job

Whatever you do, work at it with all your heart, as working for the Lord, not for men, since you know that you will receive an inheritance from the Lord as a reward. It is the Lord Christ you are serving.

COLOSSIANS 3:23-24

When was the last time you learned something new, achieved a fresh objective, or met a new challenge on the job? Are you working below your skill level? Do you feel as though you could do your job in your sleep?

Feeling bored with our jobs is a malady that strikes all of us at times. On the other hand, ongoing dissatisfaction on the job can lead to poor work habits and deteriorating performance.

When Paul said we are to do with all our hearts whatever we do, as for the Lord, that included even a job that seems boring. Here are some suggestions to help overcome that bored feeling:

- Look for new ways to do what you've been doing. Get creative. Take some risks. Find different—perhaps better— methods and techniques that will engage your mind, relieve the boredom, and maybe even improve your performance.

- If a certain task requires little thought, use the time to memorize Scripture, pray for people, or meditate. In some work situations, you may even be able to listen to books on tape or other edifying recordings (using earphones).

- Ask your supervisor for more responsibility. Suggest additional tasks you would like to do.

These are just a few suggestions, but the important thing is to remember that you are serving the Lord Christ, and therefore the job should be done to the best of your ability, even if it is boring. Even boring jobs will be rewarded in heaven, if you do the job for the Lord.

Today's Challenge
To remember that my job performance matters to God, and to look for creative ways to relieve the boredom.

Today's Prayer
Lord, you see everything I do, and I want to please you even in the most mundane aspects of my work life. Give me a fresh enthusiasm for the work you have given me to do today.

TEN

—❦—

Learning to Persevere

You need to persevere so that when you have done the will of
God, you will receive what he has promised.

HEBREWS 10:36

Have the pressures of your job ever built up so much that you
wanted to quit? If so, you're in good company; even King
David admitted to feeling like this. In Psalms 55:6 we read:
"Oh, that I had the wings of a dove! I would fly away and be at
rest."

But the writer of the book of Hebrews gives us another
choice to help us work through occasional bouts of discouragement. Hebrews 12:13 says, "Don't wander away from the path
but forge steadily onward. On the right path the limping foot
recovers strength and does not collapse."

How often are we tempted to quit as soon as we develop a
limp? Maybe that first attempt failed, or the resources you were
counting on didn't come through, or you ran into some other
obstacle. But the Bible tells us to keep going on the right path,
even with our limps.

It's not always easy. I can remember saying, "What use is
it, Lord? I don't see light at the end of the tunnel, and I'd
just like to walk away from the whole thing." If you have
those kinds of thoughts you might as well talk to God about
them. He knows what you're thinking anyway. But the
writer of Hebrews tells us to persevere in order that we may

be spiritually mature and complete.

God is looking for people with endurance. Quitters don't win and winners don't quit. Let's stick to it, and make it to the finish line by his grace.

Today's Challenge

To be found faithful to what God has called me to do, even when I want to quit.

Today's Prayer

Lord, I want to be a faithful servant of Jesus Christ. Help me today to persevere in what you've given me to do. Help me to remember that there are bad days and good days, but the person who wins doesn't quit on the bad days.

ELEVEN

— ❧ —

Warn the Idle

And we urge you, brothers, warn those who are idle, encourage the timid, help the weak, be patient with everyone.

1 THESSALONIANS 5:14

Habitually avoiding work is never acceptable to God. In fact, idleness is strongly condemned by our Lord himself. In the parable of the talents, the idle servant who did nothing with his one talent was condemned by his master as a "wicked, lazy servant" (see Matthew 25:14-30).

Consider Ecclesiastes 10:18, which says that if someone is lazy, "the rafters sag; if his hands are idle, the house leaks." Idleness leads to disaster. Not using the time and resources God has given us will eventually cause our world to crumble around us. If you tend to struggle with idleness and laziness but do not make an effort to change this pattern, you're going to find yourself bombarded with all kinds of problems.

Physical idleness and laziness can lead to deterioration of your assets and property, loss of income, and loss of jobs or career opportunities. Spiritual idleness and laziness will lead to moral failure, loss of fellowship with the Lord, and lost opportunities to do eternally significant things.

Do you remember in the parable of the talents what happened to the guy with one talent, the wicked, lazy slave? He lost the one talent he had; it was taken away and given to the one who was not idle. The same will happen to us today if we are habitually idle. If you don't use what God has given you, you'll lose it.

Today's Challenge

To examine my own life for idleness.

Today's Prayer

Lord, I recognize that you are not soft on idleness. I want to confess any areas of idleness in my own life. Help me to be diligent, even in the small things.

TWELVE

— ∾ —

Talk to Yourself

Why are you downcast, O my soul? Why so disturbed within me? Put your hope in God, for I will yet praise him, my Savior and my God.

PSALM 42:5

In Psalm 42 the psalmist reveals feelings with which most of us can relate. Evidently he was struggling with depression, with discouragement, with the blahs, just like you and I do from time to time.

Notice how he talks to himself as a way to turn around his wrong thinking. In the fifth verse, we read, "My soul is downcast within me; therefore I will remember you...." This is a very good technique for us, as well. When we feel down, we should force ourselves to remember and recite out loud God's goodness to us in times past.

Notice something else. The psalmist did not push aside or deny his darker feelings or doubts: "Why have you forgotten me? Why have you rejected me?" He voiced these doubts and questions out loud to God, but immediately he came back to the truth of praising and hoping in God.

When I find myself doubting and questioning God, I try to voice this to him out loud. "Lord, I feel as though you're not there. I just can't understand why this has happened. I can't help but wonder if you've forgotten about me here. *But*—I know better, Lord. I remember what you've done in the past, and I know your ways are not my ways. *Therefore*, I trust you, I place my hope in you. You are my Savior and my God."

I dare not voice these doubts without ending on a note of praise. But I find that voicing them out loud forces me to hear how faithless I have become, and it drives me back to praise and trust in my God.

So, talk to yourself. I believe it's a scriptural principle we need to incorporate into our lives to help us find victory in those everyday ups and downs.

Today's Challenge

To encourage myself throughout the day with self-talk that focuses on what the Lord has done for me.

Today's Prayer

Lord, make me aware all day of my own self-talk, and help me to stay focused on you, no matter what goes wrong today. Keep me from making my day worse through my own discouraging words.

THIRTEEN

— ∽ —

Overlook an Insult

A fool shows his annoyance at once, but a prudent man overlooks an insult.

PROVERBS 12:16

Not too long ago, I discovered that someone had insulted me. They accused me—behind my back—of a lack of integrity, and I was upset. It hurt and I wanted to retaliate. I wanted to let that person know they had hurt me. I wanted to make them feel bad about it. Can you identify with these reactions?

I once read from Proverbs that a prudent person overlooks an insult. That wonderfully quiet voice inside said to me, "Mary, don't do a thing about the insult; overlook it."

"But," I thought, "that's not fair. They shouldn't be allowed to get away with it." Then once again, I heard his voice saying, "No, you must overlook it—act as though you never knew about it." That was the first thing I learned about handling an insult.

Second, I learned that I had to get it out of my mind. I found I was thinking of it continually, and it was preventing me from getting anything done, keeping me upset, doing me harm. So I had to attack the thought patterns and bring them back in line.

Then, with a little more time under my belt, I thought, "What can I learn from this insult?" And God pointed out five lessons for me. They were, briefly, be teachable, don't become jaded in God's work, guard your words carefully, never say anything behind someone's back, and don't let yourself become defensive. Lots of good reminders and lessons from one insult!

So, if you've been insulted lately, I recommend this procedure to you. Number one, overlook it. Act as though it never happened. Number two, push it out of your mind every time it starts to creep back in. And number three, ask God to teach you a specific lesson from the experience. Then the whole unpleasant episode will not have been fruitless. You will have grown and learned through it.

Today's Challenge

Not to overreact to insults, but rather to learn how to overlook them.

Today's Prayer

Lord, when someone insults me, I really have difficulty in not retaliating. Please help me today to overlook any insult that comes my way, to get it out of my head, and then to grow even through an insult.

— ∾ —

Overqualified for a Job

So the Twelve gathered all the disciples together and said, "It would not be right for us to neglect the ministry of the word of God in order to wait on tables. Brothers, choose seven men from among you who are known to be full of the Spirit and wisdom. We will turn this responsibility over to them...."

ACTS 6:2-3

Do you feel as though you're overqualified for the work you're doing? When we think the work we have to do is beneath our capabilities, our dignity, or our education, it can be hard to take.

In Acts 6 and 7 we read that the disciples were looking for seven men for a rather lowly job: waiting on tables and distributing food. It's interesting to note the qualifications they were seeking in these waiters: they had to be full of the Spirit and wisdom.

Seven men were selected, and at the top of the list was Stephen, who was described as a man full of faith and of the Holy Spirit. Wouldn't that qualify Stephen for a higher position in the church? Why didn't they give him a better title, more responsibility? After all, weren't his gifts being wasted by his waiting on tables? And yet we read that God used Stephen, doing great wonders and miraculous signs among the people through him.

God used even Stephen's death for his glory. Standing

before the Sanhedrin, Stephen preached his last sermon and was stoned to death. Yet his death was witnessed by Saul of Tarsus, who became the mighty apostle Paul, used by God to reach the Gentiles.

Suppose Stephen had not been willing to serve in a job that was beneath him. Suppose he had refused to accept the lowly position. He would have missed his destiny.

If you're overqualified for your job, maybe it's because God has something he wants you to do there that is his work. Don't miss it.

Today's Challenge

To see God's purpose for me right where I am, even when I'm overqualified for the job.

Today's Prayer

Lord, today I need to understand that you often have purposes for me that are not visible at the present time. Please help me to realize that even in a job that is "beneath me," you can use me for heavenly purposes.

FOURTEEN

— ❧ —

The Importance of an Individual

What do you think? If a man owns a hundred sheep, and one of them wanders away, will he not leave the ninety-nine on the hills and go to look for the one that wandered off? And if he finds it, I tell you the truth, he is happier about that one sheep than about the ninety-nine that did not wander off. In the same way your Father in heaven is not willing that any of these little ones should be lost.

MATTHEW 18:12-14

You remember the famous line by Linus, who says, "Lucy, I love mankind. It's people I don't like." I think we can relate to Linus. We can feel for the starving masses in Africa or the homeless in Armenia. Yet we easily ignore those all around us who desperately need a touch of God's love.

The beautiful story Jesus told of the shepherd and the lost sheep shows us how much God cares for each individual. When Jesus looked out he saw one generous young man and many individuals hungry for truth; his disciples saw a swarming mass of humanity that needed to be fed immediately and at great expense.

Jesus interrupted his schedule and his plans time and again to respond to individual requests—the man whose daughter was dying, the centurion whose servant was sick, the woman who touched his garment in a crowd to find healing. Jesus never hesitated to take time for individuals. In his economy, that is the wisest investment of time and money.

Is there someone at work whom you have been ignoring, someone who needs a listening ear? At home do you model compassion for your own children? Have you included that neglected neighborhood child in your plans? Are you avoiding that individual at church who seems to take so much of your time? Are you too busy for individuals?

Think about those individuals in your life today, and ask God to help you reach out to the ones all around you who need God's love through you.

Today's Challenge

To be aware of the individuals around me who are important to God.

Today's Prayer

Lord, make me aware today that each individual around me is important to you. Help me to see them, to care about them, and to reach out to them with your love.

— ∼ —

Humble Yourself

Humble yourselves, therefore, under God's mighty hand, that he may lift you up in due time.

1 PETER 5:6

In Numbers 12:3 Moses is identified as a "very humble man, more humble than anyone else on the face of the earth." What was it that made Moses so humble? After all, he had great power and wealth and the highest position in his country. He had spiritual privileges, talking with God face to face, and he performed incredible miracles. How could he be so humble?

Here are some things that contributed to Moses' humility. First, he spent forty years wandering in the desert because of a failure on his part. Humbling ourselves means learning that, in our own strength, we are failures.

Moses also had a speech impediment. He stuttered and couldn't give a speech, so Aaron became his spokesperson. How humbling that must have been for a great leader like Moses, a reminder that his talents and skills were not sufficient. In the same way, we can be thankful for the impediments we have in our own lives that contribute to our own humility.

The main reason Moses was able to be humble was that his highest priority was to know God. Moses knew God better than any person on earth. He spent lots of time alone with

God. When we start to focus our lives on knowing God, humility is an inevitable result. True humility is found by learning who we are in relation to who God is.

Today's Challenge

To learn to be truly humble.

Today's Prayer

Lord, show me today how and when to humble myself. Make me want to be truly humble.

SIXTEEN

— ∼ —

Be Kind

The Lord's servant must not quarrel; instead, he must be kind to everyone.

2 TIMOTHY 2:24

Do you work with someone who doesn't pull a fair share of the workload? We can have different reactions to that kind of co-worker. The first is to tell him or her a thing or two, straighten the situation out, and make that person do right! If you've tried that one, you may have discovered that it doesn't often work. A tough confrontation usually just widens the breach.

Another response is to keep your anger inside, to allow it to turn into bitterness, and to become sour and vindictive. If you never confront the co-worker who continually dumps work on you, that could be where you're headed.

A better course of action is to follow Paul's instruction to Timothy: treat that person with kindness. Yes, "everyone" includes the lazy co-worker.

What are reasonable ways to be kind to such a person? It could involve speaking the truth in love; it might mean helping that co-worker learn to do his or her job better; it may even involve leaving that person alone to face the consequences of his or her poor work habits. If you're not quite sure how to be kind, pray for guidance.

Regardless of the performance of others, you and I must

not resort to hypocritical words or faked facial expressions. We must show genuine concern for those who need a kind touch.

Today's Challenge

To be genuinely kind to that co-worker who tries my patience, whether or not I feel like doing it.

Today's Prayer

Lord, I want to obey you and please you by being kind to _____ today. Please give me a pure motivation to do that and show me how.

SEVENTEEN

— ∿ —

Fleeing Dangerous Relationships

Make level paths for your feet and take only ways that are firm.
Do not swerve to the right or the left; keep your foot from evil.

PROVERBS 4:26-27

Every sin that entraps us begins with the first step. If we are alert enough to avoid that first wrong step, we will eliminate a great deal of grief and trouble from our lives.

The most deceptive "swerves" lead people into illicit and immoral relationships. Rarely do people intentionally enter into these affairs. They often begin with what seems like an innocent conversation, a harmless lunch, a simple phone call. A compassionate heart may feel for a co-worker who is having marital difficulties, with good intentions, but without adequate wisdom.

If you work with a person of the opposite sex who is having marital difficulties, for your own protection don't get caught in the trap of becoming a sympathetic ear or a shoulder to cry on. That's where affairs often begin—and don't think it can't happen to you. That co-worker may indeed need some counsel, but you are not the appropriate person to give it. Not even a lunch; not even a phone call; not even a quiet conversation after work.

Flee from this type of relationship right away. It's a ready-made opportunity for grief and heartache, and can be totally avoided by making certain that you keep your feet on the "straight and narrow", without swerving one inch to the right or the left.

Today's Challenge
To examine every relationship with wisdom from above to determine if any danger lies ahead that can be avoided by keeping my feet firmly set on the right path.

Today's Prayer
Lord, please help me keep all my relationships with my co-workers and business contacts completely pure and honest. Help me avoid even that first small step off the path, especially when it comes to relationships.

EIGHTEEN

— ∾ —

Wholesome Words

Do not let any unwholesome talk come out of your mouths, but only what is helpful for building others up according to their needs, that it may benefit those who listen.

EPHESIANS 4:29

This verse from Paul's letter to the Ephesians is one of the most life-changing verses, if and when we seriously start to incorporate it into our everyday lives.

What are some of the unwholesome things that come out of our mouths? Office gossip would have to score high on that list, wouldn't it? Most workplaces overflow with harmful, unkind, sometimes vicious gossip. It can become so commonplace that we scarcely even react to it.

It's easy to get caught up in gossip, but as Christians we need to be very careful never to be part of such unedifying talk. Never! As a believer, you must not bad-mouth the boss, the company, or anyone else. It should be obvious that you don't partake of that unwholesome talk.

I urge you to watch those words that come out of your mouth on your job, and ask God to make them words that will benefit those who listen. That's one powerful way to make your workday count for Jesus.

Today's Challenge

To be aware of every word I say today, and to screen carefully every word so that nothing harmful or unwholesome comes out, but only words that will edify and encourage those around me.

Today's Prayer

Lord, give me a new awareness of the words I speak today. Help me to say things that will help and encourage others, and to avoid those words that will discourage or belittle anyone in any way.

— ∼ —

Avoid Envying Those Without Christ

Do not fret because of evil men or be envious of the wicked, for the evil man has no future hope, and the lamp of the wicked will be snuffed out.

PROVERBS 24:19-20

The first time I held a sales position, one of my associates was a woman of questionable morals who was on a fast track to the top. She knew how to "schmooze" with customers and managers and it seemed to work just fine for her. While I worked hard to meet my sales quota, I couldn't help but wonder why she was so favored by the higher-ups.

Is there someone in your office who knows how to "work the system" so that he or she gets maximum recognition for minimum effort? Does this person's unethical and immoral behavior seem to go unnoticed and unpunished … or, worse, explained away because it gets results?

Is there someone like that where you work? Has the green-eyed monster gotten to you yet? Have you been tempted to ask God why your hard work goes unnoticed while your co-worker's shenanigans are being rewarded?

When we envy the evil or wicked people around us—people who don't yet know Jesus as their Savior—we fall into the common trap of looking only at the here and now instead of focusing on the eternal. Proverbs 24:20 reminds us that there is no future hope for those who are without Christ. All the money and success and favor in the world cannot possibly compare with the peace and contentment we possess.

If you've been tempted to envy someone who doesn't know Jesus, remember that they have no future hope unless they are born from above. That will change your envy into compassion, and give you joy because you are so rich in Jesus.

Today's Challenge

To look beyond the success of those without Christ and see their truly desperate state, and thereby to avoid envying them.

Today's Prayer

Lord, I am sometimes tempted to wonder why those who don't know you have it so good while I struggle. I confess my sin of envy, and ask you to give me the ability to see beyond the success of this world and remember that the end for those without you is desperately dismal. I thank you that because of Jesus I am rich.

TWENTY

— ❧ —

Playing Hurt

Endure hardship with us like a good soldier of Christ Jesus.

2 TIMOTHY 2:3

If you've ever been involved with any kind of sports competition, you're familiar with the term "playing hurt." This happens when a key player who injures himself in a game continues to play in spite of the injury. They pull themselves off the floor or ground and continue for the good of the team.

Well, there are times in our lives when we also must "play hurt." Suppose someone has trampled on your feelings or been very cruel to you. It makes you want to go to the sidelines and lick your wounds, doesn't it? Your first reaction is to walk out of the game and say, "Forget it. Who needs this?"

But a true servant of Jesus Christ often has to "play hurt." Jesus is looking for people with perseverance; people who play in spite of the pain; people who stay in the game even though they might want to go sit on the bench awhile.

In Hebrews 12 we see that hardship produces discipline in our lives. Paul wrote to the Corinthians that he delighted in weaknesses and difficulties, for "when I am weak, then I am strong" (2 Cor 12:10). In Romans 5 we read that suffering produces perseverance, and perseverance produces character.

Can you think of any effective servant of God who hasn't had to "play hurt"? I can't. Are you hurt today? Well, are you going to go sit on the sidelines and lick your wounds, or will you choose to endure hardship as a good soldier would?

Today's Challenge

To be faithful and dependable and do what God has given me to do, even when I have to "play hurt."

Today's Prayer

Lord, often when I'm hurt in some way, I just want to give up. Please help me learn to be a faithful servant who endures hardship for you when I need to.

— ∽ —

TWENTY-ONE

Ready to Give an Answer

But in your hearts set apart Christ as Lord. Always be prepared to give an answer to everyone who asks you to give the reason for the hope that you have. But do this with gentleness and respect.

1 PETER 3:15

Have you ever had an opportunity to share your beliefs, and found that your mouth just wouldn't work? It can be difficult to *verbalize* our faith, especially at work.

It's true that we need to exercise good judgment in witnessing, but at the same time, we should be willing to put words to our witness when God gives us an open door. Open doors usually come in the form of questions:

"How can you put up with that person?"

"You never seem to get upset; how can you stay so calm?"

"Why are you always so positive?"

Don't be intimidated or afraid to put words to your witness when God gives you an opportunity. Even if the question comes in an exasperated form, it opens a door for an answer.

When we respond with gentleness and respect to another person, and listen patiently to his or her opinions, we may find that we ourselves have won a listening ear.

Today's Challenge

To look for opportunities to tell what Jesus means to me and why I have put my trust in him.

Today's Prayer

Lord, today help me to be ready to give a verbal answer to any question that opens a door for a witness. May I be aware of the opportunities that come my way, and may I never be ashamed to tell anyone how you have changed my life.

— ✿ —

TWENTY-TWO

Guard Against Greed

"Watch out! Be on your guard against all kinds of greed; a man's life does not consist in the abundance of his possessions."

LUKE 12:15

Greed is a word we hear quite often these days. We have become a greedy people, and that greed is eating away at the very fiber of our lives. But this greed problem is nothing new. And there certainly are many different kinds of greed.

There's greed for power, the drive to have authority and influence over other people. Many people really live for recognition from others. Of course, greed for material possessions is very commonplace. Almost daily we hear of another scandal on Wall Street or in government where greed for money has driven people to destroy their lives.

When you think about it, greed is pride. It is a desire within us to show the world who we are by our status in life, our possessions, or our fame. Greed is a direct result of the pride of life.

And greed is contagious. If you're around people who have lots of things and who focus their life on getting more and more things, you'll discover that it's very difficult not to be swept right along into that greedy mindset.

Greed is also cancerous. It grows fast, and it destroys everything it touches. No wonder Jesus said we must be on our guard against all kinds of greed. Greed can overtake us quickly and completely distort our priorities and our commitment to the Lord.

Jesus said life is more than food or clothes; it is peace and contentment. Those can't be bought; they are found only in Jesus.

Today's Challenge

To be on guard against all the greed that surrounds me, especially in the working world.

Today's Prayer

Lord, all around me are powerful currents of greed. I can be very vulnerable when greedy impulses try to drag me into a "want" mode, wanting money or power or things. Please help me, by your grace, to be victorious over all kinds of greed today.

TWENTY-THREE

— ∼ —

Don't Overdraw Your Accounts!

Do not grieve, for the joy of the Lord is your strength.
NEHEMIAH 8:10

If you have you ever tried to take more out of your bank account than you put in, you know the meaning of the term "overdrawn." Problems often arise when we take out of something more than we have put in.

When people try to take more out of relationships than they put in, the results are equally disastrous. I've seen employees who want to take out of their company more than they have invested in it. They expect their employers to provide security, good pay, and great fringe benefits, but they aren't willing to put in loyalty, hard work, and extra effort. And it works in reverse. Many employers try to take more out of their employees than they invest in them.

Many of us live fatigued, burned-out, overdrawn lifestyles because we don't deposit enough in our energy accounts to cover the checks we draw on them. The most essential daily deposit is the Word of God. Careful and consistent meditation on God's Word pours strength into our energy accounts. When we fail to make those deposits, our joy quickly taps out.

We also need personal relationships from which to gain strength. Marriage was intended by God to be a source of strength. We also need close relationships with friends and family. You don't have to have many, but you need one or two.

So, are you living in "overdrawn" mode? If so, start making the necessary deposits into your own inner bank account today.

Today's Challenge

To determine where and why I am living in "overdrawn" mode.

Today's Prayer

Lord, show me where I am failing to make the necessary deposits to give me the strength I need for the tasks in front of me. If I'm living in an overdrawn mode, please show me how to break this cycle and learn to live a balanced lifestyle.

TWENTY-FOUR

— ∾ —

Motivating Words

The wise in heart are called discerning, and pleasant words promote instruction.

PROVERBS 16:21

Are you responsible for training someone on your job? Whether you're a manager, a trainer, or an experienced co-worker, you're likely to have some training assignments, formal or informal. There are also those occasions when you must require certain performance or behavior from your employees or co-workers. How can you motivate and inspire others to do what has to be done?

Solomon advises us to use pleasant words. We still catch more flies with honey than vinegar, as they say. It's amazing how differently people react to the same message, given in different words. I can say, "I have a suggestion …" or "You've got to do this right away …", each followed by my instructions. Which words do you think will get a better response?

The New American Standard Bible translates this verse from Proverbs 16 slightly differently: "The wise in heart will be called discerning, and sweetness of speech increases persuasiveness." Sweetness of speech is the art of making your words easy to swallow. It is not hypocrisy or phoniness; it is the wisdom of thinking ahead and choosing words that create a positive rather than a negative reaction.

Whether you are a manager, trainer, or fellow employee,

remember that your choice of words can make all the difference in whether people want to follow you or not. Increase your persuasiveness and effectiveness today. Choose pleasant words that go down easily.

Today's Challenge

To give instructions and directions in the most pleasant and motivating way possible.

Today's Prayer

Lord, as I undertake to instruct, train, and direct others today, please give me the wisdom to choose words that will motivate and encourage. Teach me how to persuade through pleasant and easy-to-handle speech.

—◈—

TWENTY-FIVE

Be Angry and Sin Not

In your anger do not sin. Do not let the sun go down while you are still angry.

EPHESIANS 4:26

Whenever I feel angry, a twinge of guilt always seems to follow. And yet, anger can be a legitimate emotion and response. The Bible is full of references to the anger of God. There were several occasions when Jesus displayed obvious anger toward hypocrites and evil practices. Therefore, it is not necessarily wrong for us to be angry.

At the same time, anger is an emotion that has to be very carefully controlled. While it may not be wrong to be angry, it is wrong to rush into anger and it is wrong to harbor anger. In James 1:19-20 we read: "Everyone should be quick to listen, slow to speak, and slow to become angry, for man's anger does not bring about the righteous life that God desires."

Hasty anger will almost always be out of control and inappropriate. Harbored anger quickly develops into bitterness, malice, and all kinds of ugly things. So, two key principles from Scripture are that anger is not always wrong, but it is wrong to be easily angered and to harbor anger.

If we learn to think of these two principles when we feel angry, we'll know if it is justified or not. If we are slow to get angry, then we won't display that hot-tempered kind of anger. And if we refuse to let the sun go down while we're still angry, we'll settle those matters and keep them from turning into bitterness and malice.

The next time you feel anger flare up, think about what is causing this response. Is this emotion self-focused, from hurt feelings or a bruised ego, and is your anger directed at another person? Or is the focus of your anger on another person's unjust or immoral behavior? If you are driven to retaliate, rather than to restore the relationship, your anger may not be the "slow and righteous" kind.

Today's Challenge

To be slow to anger, and never to go to sleep angry.

Today's Prayer

Lord, sometimes I am overwhelmed with anger for the wrong reasons. Please help me to be very slow to express my anger, and then to express it appropriately. And please keep me from harboring anger.

— ❧ —

When Your Boss Belittles You

"You have heard that it was said, 'Love your neighbor and hate your enemy.' But I tell you: Love your enemies and pray for those who persecute you, that you may be sons of your Father in heaven."

MATTHEW 5:43-45

How should a Christian respond when a boss belittles him or her? Unfortunately this is a fairly common occurrence in our business world, and it puts us in a tough spot.

Our first reaction may be either to resist and strike back or to be intimidated and retreat. Neither reaction is proper. When someone demonstrates this kind of behavior, we should understand that it is usually a symptom of insecurity. Underneath the intimidating facade is often a person who can only feel good about himself or herself by making someone else look small.

A Christian has to learn to move from the self-focused reaction that is typical in these situations—"Oh, poor me. This is not fair!"—to a God-focused reaction, understanding how God sees this person. This comes only through prayer. Start praying for your boss.

I don't mean that you should pray for lightning to strike him or her, but rather that God will give you his perspective of this person. Pray that God will help you see beneath the facade and get a glimpse of why this person is this way. Pray that, in spite of the unfair treatment, you will be able to respond in Christlike ways.

Every person in your life is there through God's permissive will, and that means that God can turn tough situations into avenues of growth and learning for you, even if the other person never changes.

Today's Challenge
To pray for the boss (or anyone else) who treats me with disrespect or unfairness.

Today's Prayer
Lord, today please fill my heart with your love and help me to love those who treat me wrong. Help me to see them as you see them, and keep me from reacting in a selfish, vindictive manner.

TWENTY-SEVEN

— ∾ —

Working With Total Integrity

*The man of integrity walks securely, but he who takes crooked
paths will be found out.*

PROVERBS 10:9

Have you ever been faced with an ethical decision on the job?
Were you ever tempted to adjust those figures a bit to make
yourself look better? Or to cut a corner here and there on an
expense report to put a few extra bucks in your pocket? Or to
lie to your boss to avoid blame for a problem?

Maybe you've been asked or urged or told to do something
unethical by someone in authority. Like lying about your
boss's availability, or your product's capability, or your company's service. The ethical decision you face is a simple one;
it's not difficult to figure out what is the right thing to do. But
it may not be easy for you to make that decision because you
may indeed put yourself or your job at some risk.

Remember what Solomon taught us: When you walk in
integrity, doing what you know is the right thing to do
whether it's easy or not, your path is secure. You're on solid
ground. You don't have to lie awake at night wondering if
you'll be found out. You will walk securely.

On the other hand, if you take the crooked path, no matter
how inconsequential it may seem, you compromise your
integrity and risk your testimony for Jesus Christ. Put yourself

on a crooked path, and eventually it will be found out. Even when no one else is watching, God knows.

Today's Challenge

To make every workday one of integrity, even if my career is jeopardized.

Today's Prayer

Lord, whatever issues or decisions are placed before me today, I want to choose the right path. I want to make decisions based not just on the consequences, but on what you would want me to do. Please enable me to have the highest level of integrity in all I do this day.

— ≈ —

TWENTY-EIGHT

What Brings Out the Worst in You?

Who can discern his errors? Forgive my hidden faults. Keep your servant also from willful sins; may they not rule over me. Then will I be blameless, innocent of great transgression.

PSALM 19:12-13

Have you ever said something like, "She (or he) just brings out the worst in me!"? It really is true that certain people and certain circumstances seem to bring out the worst in us. Did you ever think that there might be a reason for that?

In this passage we see that David was aware of two kinds of sin in his life: those he had deliberately chosen to embrace, and those that were hidden so that even he could not see them in his own life.

Of course, David is not the only one to struggle with these two kinds of sin. And yet it is those hidden errors that are not always easily recognized as sinful. As David put it: "Who can discern his errors?"

God has a simple solution to pinpoint these trouble spots in our lives: people that bring out the worst in us.

Think about it: Is there a person in your life who causes you to be angry every time he or she is in your presence? Does it seem like you are always saying something hateful or unkind to that person? Perhaps God is using that person to expose a judgmental attitude, lack of compassion, or a proud spirit.

One of my regular prayers is to ask God to show me my

hidden errors. It's a good prayer, so I encourage you to pray the same way. And then every time you're around someone who brings out the worst in you, stop and realize that God is answering your prayer and showing you your hidden errors, so that you can become more Christlike.

Today's Challenge

To realize who brings out the worst in me and what God is trying to teach me through those people.

Today's Prayer

Lord, I realize that _____ brings out the worst in me. I seem to always handle things poorly with this person. Please show me what it is in me that you are trying to change. Please help me to learn from this difficult relationship how I can be more like Jesus.

—~—

TWENTY-NINE

When a Co-worker Tries to Make You Look Bad

Let your conversation be always full of grace, seasoned with salt,
so that you may know how to answer everyone.

COLOSSIANS 4:6

Have you ever worked with a person who tried to make you look bad and undermined your position with the boss, in order to make himself or herself look better? How should a Christian react in this predicament?

Of course, we should always start with prayer—lots of prayer for this person, as well as for wisdom and understanding. Prayer really helps us gain God's perspective, and without that perspective, our reactions are bound to be less than Christlike.

Next, find a way to communicate openly with this person, to confront his or her behavior. Obviously, you will need to tailor your approach to fit the circumstances of your own situation, but a few things are important to remember.

Have you ever noticed that Jesus frequently confronted people over a meal? There's something about sharing a meal together that presents a nonthreatening environment for touchy discussions. Invite this person to lunch or dinner, your treat, and see if you can open up the communication channels.

Remember that your choice of words is most critical. Give those words much thought and prayer. If you start by saying, "You know, I'm really sick and tired of the way you always try to make me look bad so you'll look good," you're not likely to have much success. However, you might promote a good communication session if you say, "You know, I think we both recognize the value of a pleasant working environment, and I want to do what I can to make that happen. I have sensed some difficulty in our working relationship, and I thought it might be helpful if we could find some common understanding that would alleviate that tension."

Finally, remember that you don't have to cover everything in one conversation. Be willing to take baby steps, and allow time to help.

Today's Challenge

To season my words of confrontation and communication with grace so that I will be successful in dealing with difficult people.

Today's Prayer

Lord, show me if and when I need to confront someone about unacceptable behavior or attitudes. Give me grace to do it in a kind way.

THIRTY

_— ∾ —_

Overcoming Fears of the Future

And my God will meet all your needs according to his glorious riches in Christ Jesus.

PHILIPPIANS 4:19

Many people are dealing with the harsh realities of layoffs and "rightsizing." Has it happened to you? Perhaps you're facing the possibility of accepting a position with less pay, or losing that overtime money, or doing without that big bonus you were counting on.

This is a good time to check out what and whom you really trust. Employment and financial insecurity can quickly reveal some hidden fears within us. Losing that security—or even just having it threatened—can make us see how much we've depended on ourselves instead of our God.

There have been nights that I've lain in my bed, sleepless, wondering where the money was going to come from to meet my needs. Those were faithless nights of panic and worry. I'm learning to go back to the basics of this wonderful verse from Philippians and remind myself that God has committed himself to take care of me and meet all of my needs. His riches in Christ Jesus are beyond measure and overflowing. Therefore, I can—and must—learn to trust him.

If you're facing job or financial insecurity today, ask God to make this a time when you learn to trust him in new ways. You may discover that this can be an incredibly meaningful time of learning to trust God.

Today's Challenge

To keep my mind focused on God's promise to take care of me and not to allow the fears of the future to overtake me.

Today's Prayer

Lord, you have promised to meet all my needs, and I know that you keep your promises. Therefore, I choose to trust you today, regardless of my circumstances. When insecurity begins to take over my mind, please help me to go back to this wonderful promise of your care and once again put my trust in you.

THIRTY-ONE

— ❧ —

Accepting Change as Opportunity for Growth

I can do everything through him who gives me strength.

PHILIPPIANS 4:13

A woman came to work for me who had never touched a computer. After forty years in the workplace, she was now faced with the challenge of learning to use a computer. I learned later that she was frightened about the prospects of learning this new technology, but she had determined in her heart that she wouldn't let a computer defeat her, and had claimed the promise that she could do all things through him who gave her strength. She was convinced Christ would give her the ability to learn to use a computer. And she did!

Change! We don't like it, do we? But in order to thrive in any work environment today, we need to be adaptable. This wonderful promise from Philippians is a great one to hold on to when facing an uncomfortable challenge.

Don't be afraid of change. Remember that you can grow only by changing, so the change you're facing could be a hidden blessing. You can trust God to give you the strength, the knowledge, the aptitude, the patience, and the attitude you need to make that needed change.

Today's Challenge

To accept change as an opportunity for growth and not be frightened or intimidated by it.

69

Today's Prayer

Lord, I sometimes have a knee-jerk reaction to change and see it as a threat. Please help me to remember that you can give me the strength to change when that change is right. Help me to have a healthy attitude toward change instead of fearing it as I sometimes do.

— ❧ —

THIRTY-TWO

Condemnation or Conviction?

Therefore, there is now no condemnation for those who are in Christ Jesus.

ROMANS 8:1

Do you know the difference between condemnation and conviction? Conviction is what we feel when God is dealing with us and we haven't yet obeyed. It's a guilty feeling that goes away as soon as you obey; with conviction, you know exactly what you should do.

Condemnation, on the other hand, feels much like conviction—except that you don't know what you are guilty of. Condemnation is false guilt that you lay upon yourself, or that you allow others to lay upon you. False guilt comes from the enemy, and it can really fool you if you're not careful, because it feels like conviction.

Have you been living under condemnation? I remember when I finally saw that for two years I had allowed someone to condemn me. I always felt guilty toward this person, but I didn't know why. I tried so hard to please her and win her approval, but nothing I did cut the mustard. With marvelous grace God revealed to me that this was false guilt and that I did not have to allow her or anyone else to condemn me. I'm in Christ Jesus, so for me there is now no condemnation!

What freedom to finally understand that! Our relationship continued for some time afterward, and her behavior didn't change. But I simply knew that I no longer had to accept her condemnation, no matter what she said or how she looked at me.

Check out your guilt feelings. If you're under conviction, get right with God. You'll be miserable until you do. If it's condemnation, memorize this verse and live in the joy that you cannot be condemned, by yourself or anyone else. Amen!

Today's Challenge

To live in the freedom of "no condemnation" and recognize the false guilt I've been carrying around.

Today's Prayer

Lord, I recognize that I've been living under a cloud of false guilt. Therefore, by faith I claim freedom. Please help me to live in this glorious freedom all day, and keep me from being victimized by condemnation from myself or from others. Thank you, Jesus.

— ∾ —

Responding With Gentle Words

A gentle answer turns away wrath, but a harsh word stirs up anger.

PROVERBS 15:1

Do you ever have to deal with customers who are demanding and unkind? Or co-workers who just love to argue? Or managers who bark orders instead of issuing instructions? Harsh words definitely stir up my anger, and I imagine they have a similar effect on you.

These are moments that test our self-control. If we allow anger directed at us to control our response, we will have allowed a rude person to pull us down to his or her level. That means, of course, that he or she wins, even though he or she was wrong and we were right! It doesn't seem fair, but that's how it works.

Offering a gentle answer, however, has the same effect as a slow leak in a balloon. Just as the air gradually leaking from a balloon prevents a sudden loud pop, so a gentle word turns aside the force of an angry word.

Gentle answers often begin with empathetic statements such as: "I can understand how you feel," ... "Well, it's no wonder you're upset," ... or "There's obviously been a misunderstanding; let me see what I can do." But sometimes you may need to be more creative in finding a "gentle answer"; it may involve changing the subject, or ignoring the harsh words and trying to help that person instead.

Gentle answers let others off the hook. Gentle answers relinquish the desire to strike back. Gentle answers accept some blame, regardless of who's right. Keep your words gentle and kind. Not only does this work well in defusing a difficult encounter, but also saves you a lot of time and energy.

Today's Challenge

To avoid responding to harsh, unkind words in like fashion, giving a gentle, reasoned response instead.

Today's Prayer

Lord, if today I encounter harsh words, whether from customers, co-workers, managers, friends, or family, please give me quick control of my tongue so that I do not respond in an angry way, even though I may feel angry. Please give me the grace to use words that are gentle, words that will calm and defuse rather than add fuel to the fire.

— ∾ —

Living a Life of Purity

Don't let anyone look down on you because you are young, but set an example ... in speech, in life, in love, in faith and in purity.

1 TIMOTHY 4:12

Is there an abundance of impurity in your workplace? If so, you're not alone. The conversations, the jokes, and the attitudes of those with whom you work may not meet biblical standards of purity and nobility.

We should never be intimidated by inappropriate talk and behavior, or hesitate to voice our opposition to it. Yet the best "sermon" we could preach is our own example. Our own speech and lifestyle should reflect the standard of purity we want others to observe.

While we may not curse or tell smutty jokes, we can still become a part of impure speech. For example, when was the last time you found yourself casually discussing questionable television programs and movies over morning coffee, without voicing any opposition to the "mature themes" portrayed? This kind of behavior gives tacit approval to a less-than-pure lifestyle.

Frankly, my heart often aches to see how easily even committed, Bible-loving Christians let down their standards of purity. Our testimony will never be as strong as it should be if our lives are not above reproach, both in our words and our actions. "What would Jesus do?" has become a popular phrase among young people, but it's a good question for us as well. The next time you are tempted to cut moral corners a bit in order to fit in better, ask yourself: what would Jesus do in this situation? That is our standard.

Today's Challenge

To repent of any area of impurity in my own life, and when appropriate to be willing to take a strong stand against impurity where I work.

Today's Prayer

Lord, help me to set a good example of a wholesome lifestyle. May my words, my body language, my manner of dress, my actions, and my attitudes all reflect your standards of purity. Help me never to be ashamed to take a stand against impurity, but to do so with a loving attitude.

THIRTY-FIVE

Make Choices and Decisions With Forever Eyes

So we fix our eyes not on what is seen, but on what is unseen.
For what is seen is temporary, but what is unseen is eternal.

2 CORINTHIANS 4:18

Do you know what "Forever Eyes" are? It's a term I use to remind me to look at everything from an eternal perspective. It is so easy to get preoccupied with computers, deadlines, to-do lists, event planning, housecleaning ... ad infinitum! Yet a world of unseen things is all around us, a world that is not only very real, but eternal. They are the things that last forever. I need "Forever Eyes" to see them.

"Forever Eyes" are important when it comes to establishing priorities. Perhaps the greatest challenge we face is finding and keeping a proper balance between our jobs, our home responsibilities, our church activities, and all the other hats we have to wear. When you forget to put on your "Forever Eyes," you can make some poor choices about the priorities of your life.

A very successful businesswoman recently wrote me to say that her accomplishments seemed to be having a negative effect on her marriage and home. "Forever Eyes" would remind her that healthy marriages and children are far more important to God than successful careers. If one has to be sacrificed for the other, for a Christian this is an open and shut case: your home and marriage come first.

Do you need "Forever Eyes" today? You may not always

like what you see; it may involve changing the plans you've made, or making a difficult choice. But let me assure you that God's way is better than ours. Ask him to help you live each day with eternity in mind.

Today's Challenge

To see my priority choices and decisions through "Forever Eyes," and to make choices with that perspective in mind.

Today's Prayer

Lord, I really want to choose the things that will matter in eternity. Help me remember to look through "Forever Eyes" when I'm faced with a decision concerning my priorities. I truly believe that your way is best for me.

— ∾ —

THIRTY-SIX

What Do I Smell Like?

For we are to God the aroma of Christ among those who are being saved and those who are perishing. To the one we are the smell of death; to the other, the fragrance of life.

2 CORINTHIANS 2:15-16

Have you noticed how some people like a certain perfume, while others can't stand it? That's why there are hundreds— probably thousands—of fragrances on the market, so everybody can find one they like.

But did you ever think of yourself as a perfume that is being spread everywhere? That's what Paul told the Corinthians. The aroma of Christ—his lingering presence—is beautiful to some people, but to others it is repugnant. It's difficult for me to believe that anything about Christ could be less than attractive and winsome to anyone, but the facts are, to those who are perishing his "aroma" may be offensive.

The difference in reactions can be attributed to whether or not the "smeller" has a seeking heart. Anyone who has a desire to know God will like the aroma of Christ on you. Anyone who has set their heart or mind against God will not.

So, as you go out into your world today, remember that you have no control over the effects of your aroma. Your responsibility and mine is to spread everywhere the perfume of Christ through God-controlled attitudes, actions, and words.

Today's Challenge

To make certain that the aroma I produce is a Christlike perfume, and then, to expect both positive and negative reactions to it.

Today's Prayer

Lord, I want to spread your beautiful aroma to everyone I interact with today. Help me to do that through my words, my actions, and my attitudes. If there is someone in my path today who is searching for you, I pray that the aroma of Christ in me will help them find their way to you. And if there are those who are antagonistic toward your love, give me patience and understanding to deal with them in loving ways.

— ∾ —

THIRTY-SEVEN

Help the Weak

And we urge you, brothers, warn those who are idle, encourage the timid, help the weak, be patient with everyone.

1 THESSALONIANS 5:14

Psalm 41:1 says "Blessed is he who has regard for the weak; the Lord delivers him in times of trouble." And Psalm 82:3 tells us to "defend the cause of the weak and fatherless; maintain the rights of the poor and oppressed."

Who are the weak that we are supposed to help? Well, first, those who are weak in body. Certainly that would include the elderly, sick, shut-ins, and the physically challenged. God is honored when we help those who can't do things for themselves; when we share our body's strength and stamina with those who don't have that kind of energy.

Most of us have someone in our lives that fits this category. How much do we do for those who are physically weak? I believe God is pleased when we go out of our way for these people. There are any number of ways we can help people who are not as physically strong as we are. We can visit nursing homes, hold a door for someone who is navigating with a wheelchair, or go shopping for someone who is elderly, just to mention a few. We need to help those who are physically weak.

The weak are also those who are poor and oppressed by others. There are people who need our financial help, because they cannot provide for themselves. I imagine you can think of someone right now who fits that description. This means sharing our resources with people who have less than we do— in a way that does not make them feel like "charity cases."

Maybe there's a weak co-worker on your job who needs help. He or she may be weak in technical knowledge, weak in intellect, weak in experience, or weak in know-how. How might you help that person today?

Today's Challenge

To help someone today who is weak, either physically, financially, or intellectually, not because it makes *me* feel good but because it pleases God.

Today's Prayer

Lord, please bring to my mind someone who is weak that I can help today. Show me what you want me to do for that person. Give me a compassionate heart that is sensitive to the needs of other people.

—∿—

THIRTY-EIGHT

Being Sidetracked?

You were running a good race. Who cut in on you and kept you from obeying the truth?

GALATIANS 5:7

Sometimes people start to follow the Lord, and allow him to control their lives, but later seem to lose steam and drop out of the race. Has this happened to anyone you know?

Running a race successfully requires that we be single-minded in our pursuit. Many of us start that way, but soon other things invade our thinking and steal our time and commitment. They may not be bad things; they may seem very harmless indeed. But these distractions can keep us from running our race in top form.

A common sidetrack I've noticed in myself and in others is ambition—trying to climb higher and higher on the career ladder and, in the process, allowing that ambition to sidetrack our spiritual life.

Another common sidetrack is a wrong relationship. How often people give up on the race because of someone in their life who's not on the same track. They get off course just to go and march in another person's parade.

The distraction can be something as innocent as too much television, a poor choice of reading material, or even a lack of discipline in your life. Think for a moment: have you allowed someone or something to cut in on you and keep you from being all God wants you to be? Believe me, whatever it is, it's not worth it.

It does take discipline and sacrifice to run a race to the end, but the prize is worth it. The prize is to hear our Savior say, "Well done, good and faithful servant." Like Jesus, we all want to be able to say to our Father in heaven, "I finished the work you gave me to do." That won't happen if we're easily sidetracked.

Today's Challenge

To discern whether I have allowed anything to keep me from running the race God has for me.

Today's Prayer

Lord, I am so easily sidetracked. Help me to be single-minded when it comes to doing your will. Remind me today of what is truly important, and give me the power to make decisions that will accomplish your best plans for my life.

THIRTY-NINE

— ∾ —

God Is Not Involved in Coverups

There is nothing concealed that will not be disclosed, or hidden that will not be made known.

MATTHEW 10:26

God is never involved in coverups of any kind. God has never been a part of any activity to suppress the truth, to put a good light on a bad scene, or to camouflage the truth about sin, even in the lives of his children. Especially in the lives of his children.

There are many examples in Scripture where God exposed the sin and corruption of his people. The first one that comes to mind is King David, who is described as a man after God's own heart. Yet, God did not move one finger to cover up for David when he committed adultery and murder. In fact, God made sure it came out in the open. You see, God was far more interested in King David's spiritual condition than he was in what people would think when they heard what had happened.

We've all been troubled by the revealed sin of people who have appeared to be great Christian leaders and teachers. We ask, "Why did God allow this to be exposed and do such damage to the reputation and the name of Christianity?"

Remember: God created the universe. The Creator doesn't look to his creation for affirmation or approval. Furthermore, God knows that "hidden" sin causes great corruption, just as an infected sore sends poison throughout the whole body if it is simply bandaged and never cleaned out.

Are there any coverups in your life? Things you keep sweeping under the rug, hoping no one notices, thinking you've got them under control? Remember, God will never be part of any coverup, whether you're a nationally known evangelist or a little-known Christian living in comparative obscurity.

Pick up the rug today and expose the coverup yourself. Let the blood of Christ cleanse you completely. Know freedom from the guilt of any coverup in which you're now involved.

Today's Challenge
To confess and forsake any coverup in my life at this moment.

Today's Prayer
Lord, I'm aware that you are more interested in my spiritual growth than you are in protecting me from embarrassment. I want to confess coverups in my life, where I've been trying to sweep things under the rug. Please forgive me and help me to keep the slate clean with you.

FORTY

— ❧ —

When Your Boss Treats You Unfairly

Do not repay anyone evil for evil. Be careful to do what is right in the eyes of everybody. If it is possible, as far as it depends on you, live at peace with everyone. Do not take revenge, my friends, but leave room for God's wrath, for it is written: "It is mine to avenge; I will repay," says the Lord.

ROMANS 12:17-19

How do you deal with a person, particularly a boss, who treats you unfairly or with disrespect? Resolving the problem may be easier than you think—if you are willing to make this person an object of concentrated, daily prayer. Your own attitude toward this person may change as a result of your prayers, and that in turn may change his or her attitude and tactics toward you.

On the other hand, the situation may escalate to the point that you need to confront that other person. Before you do so, however, be certain that you check out your motives carefully. Are you simply trying to be vindictive? Are you reacting out of self-pity? Are you fighting for your rights? Those are not biblically based motivations. Jesus frequently confronted people, but he always did it for their own good, not to vindicate himself.

Before you confront someone, bathe the situation in prayer and ask for God's wisdom, that the situation may be resolved at the right time and in the right way. Be careful not to overreact, and don't confront when you're emotionally upset. God may have good purposes for having you endure that unfair situation for a period of time to bring glory to him. Perhaps others may be watching you, knowing the unfairness of the situation. Your Christlike response could be a very effective witness. We must be willing to allow God to use us in this way.

Today's Challenge

To respond to unfair treatment with patience and lack of vengeance, and to confront only after prayer and careful evaluation of my motives.

Today's Prayer

Lord, please give me the strength to endure any unfair treatment that may come my way today. Also, please give me the wisdom to know when the situation should be confronted, how and when to do that, and the grace to do it in a loving way.

FORTY-ONE

— ∼ —

Complain to the Lord

I cry aloud to the Lord; I lift up my voice to the Lord for mercy. I pour out my complaint before him; before him I tell my trouble.

PSALM 142:1-2

King David had some complaints, but he knew where to go with them. He poured them out before the Lord. A few verses later in this same psalm, he went on to say, "No one is concerned for me. I have no refuge, no one cares for my life" (verse 4). Notice how David tells God exactly how he feels.

Do you ever verbalize your complaints to the Lord? You should, because he understands you, he cares about you, he's always there to listen, and he has answers. Instead of complaining to everyone around you, why not tell the one Person who invites you to bring all your cares and problems to him, because he cares for you?

I notice as David spelled out his complaint to God, he heard his own words, and that led him back into right thinking. He says in verses 5-7, "I cry to you, O Lord; I say, 'You are my refuge, my portion in the land of the living,... Set me free from my prison, that I may praise your name.'"

I find that when I pour out my complaints to God, I start to gain perspective, and I realize that my problems are not as big as I thought they were. I also realize that I'm a captive to my own complaining spirit, and once I see that, then God can set me free from the prison of griping and complaining.

Complaining is very commonplace today, especially in the working world. If you hear other people complaining all the time, you can let them drag you down to their level. Stop and think about it. Are you a complaining person? Start taking your complaints to the Lord.

Today's Challenge
To take my complaints to the Lord—not to anyone else!

Today's Prayer
Lord, please remind me throughout the day that I can express my true feelings to you at anytime without condemnation, and you will hear, understand, and help me. Please keep me from complaining to anyone else throughout this entire day.

FORTY-TWO

— ∽ —

Unanswered Questions

About the ninth hour Jesus cried out in a loud voice, "Eloi, Eloi, lama sabachthani?"—which means, "My God, my God, why have you forsaken me?"

MATTHEW 27:46

This is one of the greatest unanswered questions of all history. Jesus screamed this question to his Father in anguish, in pain—could it have been even in anger? It pierces the air around; a wail of despair thrown at God.

And yet, Jesus knew the answer. He had told his disciples many times exactly what would happen: death, burial, and resurrection. He wrestled with and settled the issue in Gethsemane the night he was arrested: "Not my will but thine be done."

Why did Jesus ask this question on the cross? He knew there was no other way. But because his agony was so intense at that moment, there was nothing else he could do except cry out, even though he already knew the answer to his question.

Many times when we are in pain our faith compels us to believe that there is a plan and purpose for our plight, and that beyond the pain will be a resurrection day. Yet in the midst of our pain we cry out with unanswerable questions. We wail. We despair.

God knows our hearts, as he knew Jesus' heart. He understands that though we ask, we do not doubt. Though we are puzzled, we will not run. In our great pain the cries will come, but underneath are his everlasting arms, and we know that the cross we are experiencing is not the end!

Jesus knew the reason for the cross, but at that moment of separation from God, he simply cried out in pain. And God, who did not answer, understood. And he understands you and me when we cry out in pain.

Today's Challenge

To take my pain to the Lord, while continuing to trust a trustworthy God.

Today's Prayer

Lord, remind me today that when I have unanswered questions, I can cry out in pain without being judged or reprimanded. Also, please let me never compromise my trust in you, no matter what pain I must endure.

FORTY-THREE

—∽—

Appropriately Assertive

The wise in heart will be called discerning, and sweetness of
speech increases persuasiveness.

PROVERBS 16:21, NASB

Have you ever wondered if it is appropriate for a Christian
woman to be assertive on her job? In the Bible we see many
examples of assertive women. There was Deborah, who was
chosen by God to lead her army into battle. That certainly
required a great deal of assertiveness. Then there was Esther,
who courageously asserted herself and saved her people
from annihilation. The woman described in Proverbs 31
could never have accomplished all she did without being
assertive, and it did not conflict with her family duties or ruin
her testimony. Lydia is a New Testament example of an
assertive businesswoman. Through her home the gospel
spread to the continent of Europe.

All of these women were admirable, respected women,
operating with God's approval and blessing—and all were
assertive. Surely we can conclude from their examples that
assertiveness is not out of place for a Christian woman, any
more than it is for a Christian man. It is not so much a male-
female issue as it is a question of following biblical standards.

I remember when the Lord first gave me this verse from
Proverbs for a particular situation on my job. I felt as though
I were being "run over," and I kept trying to change the situa-

tion by being more forceful. Before I realized it, I had assumed an adversarial role, and my powers of persuasiveness became less and less effective.

Then I came across this verse: "Sweetness of speech increases persuasiveness." "Sweetness" here does not mean saying things that are gushy, coy, or emotional, but rather, easy to swallow, palatable. As soon as I concentrated on finding ways to make my ideas palatable, I started to win. I became more assertive and more persuasive.

Today's Challenge

To be a biblically assertive woman, learning when and how to exert persuasiveness through "sweetness of speech."

Today's Prayer

Lord, I know that if I follow your principles, I can be appropriately assertive and I can positively influence those I work with and for. Please teach me today to follow your Spirit's guidance and help me to find that "sweet speech" that will increase my powers of persuasion.

— ∼ —

When Your Company's Policies Are Wrong

Everyone must submit himself to the governing authorities, for there is no authority except that which God has established.

ROMANS 13:1

A woman wrote to ask me for some advice concerning her work situation. Her company is very production-oriented, and they have strict guidelines about working quickly, taking many calls, handling questions fast, and getting off the phone in order to take more calls. The number and length of their calls are monitored and reported, and much pressure is applied to work very fast.

She felt that in doing this, she was forced to treat callers somewhat abruptly, not really helping them like she should, and this was quite frustrating to her. But her management was not impressed with her desire to answer each call completely and thoroughly; their only interest was productivity.

There may be many situations where we feel our company is not running the business in the most customer-oriented way, and we'd like to do it better, but the guidelines get in our way. Should a Christian do it the way we think it should be done, or follow instructions?

Unfortunately, many companies operate without a real customer orientation. That is symptomatic of not only a lack of human care and concern, but also a lack of good business sense. However, as long as the instructions you're given are not dishonest or illegal, you should give strong consideration to following instructions. After all, you're the employee; your employers have the right to run their company as they please, even if they choose to run it into the ground. But we also need to look for opportunities to try to change the system, if we can.

Today's Challenge

To look for ways to improve the quality of my work without compromising the amount of work I do.

Today's Prayer

Lord, I recognize my obligation to submit myself to the authorities over me. Help me to know how to change a system that needs to be changed for the better, while at the same time showing respect for those who have authority over me.

FORTY-FIVE

Job Prerequisite: Love

And now these three remain: faith, hope and love. But the greatest of these is love.

1 CORINTHIANS 13:13

Just before returning to heaven, Jesus asked Peter three questions: Do you truly love me? Do you truly love me? Do you truly love me? Jesus doesn't repeat himself without a reason, and surely he was making a pointed effort to demonstrate to Peter—and to us—the basic requirement for discipleship: loving Jesus.

If we love Jesus, everything follows in its rightful place. Why do so many of us find it difficult to live by Christian principles? Because we don't truly love Jesus very much. Why are so many Christians self-absorbed, wallowing in self-pity, never seeming to find ways out of their problems? Because their love for Jesus is anemic.

We desperately need to get back to the basics of loving Jesus, just simply focusing our lives on loving him. That's the last instruction Jesus gave to Peter, and I believe for us today it is the sum total of where we'll find our strength, our joy, our contentment, our power for service.

Don't worry about your gifts; just love Jesus. No matter what your résumé looks like, if you love Jesus—truly love him with the highest priority—you are qualified to serve him. Regardless of your IQ or your education, if you really love

Jesus, you can go to the head of the class in discipleship.

Wherever you are today, if you will focus your energies on loving Jesus, you'll discover it makes an incredible difference in your attitude, your perspective, and your effect on others.

Today's Challenge
To focus my entire day on truly loving Jesus and staying in first love with him.

Today's Prayer
Lord, it is very easy for me to love myself more than anything or anyone else, but with all my heart I want to love you, Lord. Please help me today to truly love you as I ought to.

FORTY-SIX

Suffering With a Clear Conscience

Keep a clear conscience, so that those who speak maliciously against your good behavior in Christ may be ashamed of their slander. It is better, if it is God's will, to suffer for doing good than for doing evil.

1 PETER 3:16-17

Have you ever suffered for doing good in your workplace? A friend of mine once refused to falsify some government reports as instructed by his employer, and lost his job as a result. He was unemployed for quite a few months before finding another job, causing his family financial hardship. He suffered for doing good.

I think of another woman who was caught cheating on the books where she worked. She had actually filtered out money for herself and it eventually caught up with her. She lost her job, too, but she suffered for doing evil.

Suffering is never enjoyable, whether you're suffering for doing good or for doing evil. But there is a great reward for those who do God's will, who do the right thing regardless of the personal cost, and who suffer for doing so. Peter goes on to tell us, "So then, those who suffer according to God's will should commit themselves to their faithful Creator and continue to do good" (1 Pt 4:19).

So, if you're suffering slander or malicious treatment on your job, make sure it's for doing good, not evil. And if you are suffering for doing good, take joy that you are counted worthy to share in the suffering of Christ, and "continue to do good," regardless of the consequences.

Today's Challenge
To do the right thing and always follow God's principles on my job, even if it brings some suffering into my life.

Today's Prayer
Lord, please give me the courage to be willing to suffer for doing good if that ever becomes necessary. My natural instincts cause me to try to avoid suffering. But if I must endure hardship, by your grace I want to suffer for doing good, not evil. Please help me.

— ❧ —

FORTY-SEVEN

Spiritual Productivity

For if you possess these qualities [faith, goodness, knowledge, self-control, perseverance, godliness, brotherly kindness, and love] in increasing measure, they will keep you from being ineffective and unproductive in your knowledge of our Lord Jesus Christ.

2 PETER 1:8

God has given us the character qualities listed above to help us measure the level of productivity and effectiveness in our spiritual life. For example, are you kinder this month than last month? Is your goodness more evident this year than last year? That's the test to see if you are a productive and effective Christian.

What causes unproductivity and ineffectiveness in Christians? Matthew 13:22 says that the worries of this life and the deceitfulness of wealth choke out the Word of God in our lives, making them unfruitful. It could be money worries, or worries about whom you're going to marry or how high you're going to climb on your career ladder.

I see so many Christians who know the Word of God but are never productive or effective because their minds are possessed with the worries of this life. Others are deceived by wealth, fooled by the allure of money. Whether they have it or not, they are deceived into believing that achieving financial security is essential, or that having more money will solve their problems. So no matter how much they hear the Word of

God, they are unfruitful and unproductive in their Christian walk.

Use this "character yardstick" to see how you measure up in productivity and effectiveness: (1) Are you wrapped up in non-eternal things, the worries of this world? (2) Are you deceived by money and its false promise to meet all your needs?

Today's Challenge

To examine my life and determine my level of spiritual productivity. Am I growing in faith, goodness, knowledge, self-control, perseverance, and godliness?

Today's Prayer

Lord, I don't want to stagnate spiritually. I know that I need to possess these qualities in increasing measure so that I am effective and productive for you. Please show me where I miss the mark, and help me to grow in these graces.

— ❧ —

FORTY-EIGHT

Impose Discipline

He who ignores discipline despises himself, but whoever heeds correction gains understanding.

PROVERBS 15:32

I find myself trapped in this human dilemma: I have a strong drive to accomplish and achieve, but I am not a naturally disciplined person. I am learning a very important lesson: Lack of discipline is self-inflicted suffering! If I refuse to impose discipline on myself, I will inflict suffering on myself.

What I've also learned is that when I start to lose discipline in one area of my life, it spills over to others. For example, if I let down my discipline and eat all kinds of things today that I know I shouldn't eat, I'm likely to skip the exercise program tomorrow because I'll think, "Well, what's the use of exercising after I ate all that pie yesterday?!"

Where is your discipline weak? Is it eating habits, exercise, organization, time management, laziness, or procrastination? Choose one—just one—and begin a prayer campaign. Admit to God your weakness when it comes to discipline in that area and ask for strength.

Then design some gimmicks or structures that force the discipline on you. Ask for help; tell people what you're doing so you can be held accountable. That will help to impose discipline. Then, just do it! Start today! You will discover that adding discipline to your life is indeed the road to real life.

You'll get rid of guilt, feel good about yourself, and know that you're using your gifts, time, and energy as God wants you to.

To acquire a disciplined life, we will have to pay a price. But it's a big bargain. Go for it!

Today's Challenge

To choose one area of my life where I need more discipline, and begin a campaign to acquire the needed discipline.

Today's Prayer

Lord, in this area of _____, I need to be more disciplined. Please help me every day to strengthen my resolve so that I am no longer a victim of my own lack of discipline, and so my life brings glory to you.

FORTY-NINE

— ∼ —

Thoughts and Words

May the words of my mouth and the meditation of my heart be pleasing in your sight, O Lord, my Rock and my Redeemer.

PSALMS 19:14

David's prayer is one we should all pray frequently, because our meditations—the things we think about—very much determine the words that come out of our mouth, and the words that come out of our mouth greatly affect the thoughts in our head.

We know from the book of James and many passages in Proverbs that our words are very powerful. They certainly have a great impact on other people, but they also have a great impact on us, because we hear ourselves talk. Those words are then fed back into our mental computers, which form our thoughts. Words are simply the vocal expression of what we're already thinking.

Do you often say things like: "I can't do this!" "She makes me so angry!" "This job is rotten!" or "I hate the way I look!"? If you're saying a lot of negative or inappropriate words, they will go back into your mind and cause you to think inappropriately. That thinking will produce more poor words, and those words are not pleasing in God's sight.

Try to analyze the type of thoughts you have during those moments of free thinking time. Do they tend to be encouraging thoughts, or are they downers? Do you think fearfully?

Do you imagine bad things that may happen? Are your thoughts within the guidelines of Philippians 4: true, noble, right, pure, lovely, admirable? If not, the meditations of your heart are not pleasing in God's sight.

We really need to watch our words and our thoughts carefully, and pray daily that they will be pleasing to God. Remember how closely they are connected.

Today's Challenge

To listen to myself talk and be aware of how I'm thinking today. To determine by God's grace to change my wrong patterns of talking and thinking, so that they will be pleasing in God's sight.

Today's Prayer

Lord, may the words of my mouth and the meditation of my heart be pleasing in your sight today. Please make me very aware of my thoughts and my words and how each influences the other.

FIFTY

— ∾ —

Trivialities of Life

And whatever you do, whether in word or deed, do it all in the name of the Lord Jesus, giving thanks to God the Father through him.

COLOSSIANS 3:17

For a Christian, I think the best definition of a triviality is anything that has no eternal significance. Now, there's no way to rid our lives of trivialities completely. We have to brush our teeth and make coffee, chitchat with friends and co-workers, get the mail, and take the clothes to the cleaners. These are trivial things, but they are a large part of our everyday lives.

However, some people are tormented by trivialities. They fret and fuss about those things that have no eternal significance, and are easily upset if something trivial goes wrong.

If the trivialities of life get to you too easily, ask God to make you aware of what is trivial and what is not. When I catch myself becoming upset or consumed by some triviality, I ask myself, "Mary, what difference will this make in twenty-four hours?" I find that a majority of the trivialities tormenting me won't make a bit of difference tomorrow. This really helps me to recognize trivialities quickly so I can laugh at them, turn them over to the Lord, and forget them.

As believers we have the unbelievable ability to turn trivialities into eternal happenings. How? Use those short conversations to give someone a pat on the shoulder, a word of encouragement, a small compliment. While you're doing those trivial duties, sing songs to encourage yourself, memorize Scripture, listen to good tapes. When you're driving along with your family, turn the conversation to wholesome and encouraging topics. These kinds of things transform otherwise trivial happenings into eternally significant moments.

Today's Challenge

To turn the trivialities of my life into opportunities for encouragement, for growth, for things eternally significant.

Today's Prayer

Lord, help me to remember today that I can turn the trivialities of my life into things of eternal value by doing everything for your glory. Help me not to get so caught up in these trivialities that I lose sight of what is truly important.

— ∼ —

Running Away

Take care of yourselves; don't throw away all the labor that has been spent on you, but persevere till God gives you your reward.

2 JOHN 8, PHILLIPS

Would you love to catch the next flight to some forgotten island and leave no forwarding address? Maybe your job is driving you crazy: having to deal with a difficult boss or co-worker, or having too much work to do.

Perhaps you're having troubles with relationships; they can make you want to run away. Maybe it's your spouse, or your child, or some other family member. Maybe even a close friend or a romantic relationship. Or maybe you have financial worries that make you want to run away.

Well, whatever it is that's giving you the runaway blues, I want you to know you're not alone. I remember a time when I begged God to let me out of a job I was in. I wanted out so badly, I thought I couldn't take another day. But God made it clear to me that he had a purpose in keeping me there awhile longer, and finally I agreed to submit and stay there until his time was up.

I look back now and see why—I needed to learn many spiritual lessons in that spot, and now I wouldn't take anything for those lessons. There were people I met during that time whose friendships I continue to cherish. And, like icing on the cake, the business knowledge I gained by hanging in for another two years gave me the resources and experience I needed to start up my radio ministry.

Most of us give up just before the victory! And when we do, we waste all the hard work and effort that have been poured into our lives. I want to encourage you today to persevere. Will it be easy? No. But God will give you your reward if you hang in there. Say with King David that instead of running away you will "cast your cares on the Lord," because "he will sustain you; he will never let the righteous fall" (Ps 55:22).

Today's Challenge

To persevere and "hang in there" even though everything in me wants to walk away from it all.

Today's Prayer

Lord, give me the patience to endure so that I don't throw away all the good things you've done in my life. Please help me to persevere.

— ∿ —

FIFTY-TWO

A Critical Heart

"Do not judge, or you too will be judged. For in the same way you judge others, you will be judged, and with the measure you use, it will be measured to you."

MATTHEW 7:1-2

I'm pretty quick with criticism. I can size people up before they open their mouths. And yet, I always want people to give me a break. *Can't you understand that I'm busy, and that's why I didn't speak to you? Don't you see how tired I am, and that's why I look so bad? Surely you realize that I have an appointment in ten minutes and I can't be late?*

Jesus has given us some very practical and important directives about being critical and judgmental. If we want people to give us a break and not jump to unfair conclusions, we've got to do the same for them.

Often we judge people by their bad moments and then we keep that image with us at all times. Think about your rushed days and bad moments—would you want your reputation to be damaged because someone saw you at a bad time and kept that impression of you uppermost in his or her mind?

If we want others to be kind in their judgments of us, to give us a break, then we must extend the same privilege to them. A judgmental, critical spirit is anything but Christlike. Hold your critical thoughts and tongue today; tell yourself you probably don't know the whole story; choose instead to think something positive. Remember, every time you choose to judge someone else, you are heaping judgment on yourself.

Today's Challenge
To be a nonjudgmental person instead of criticizing and finding fault in others so easily.

Today's Prayer
Lord, I know that my heart needs to abandon its tendency to criticize and blame and judge others; more often than not, my judgment is not accurate. Help me to become a loving person, and teach me to look for the positive in other people.

FIFTY-THREE

— ∽ —

Inquire of the Lord

The men of Israel sampled their provisions but did not inquire of the Lord. Then Joshua made a treaty of peace with them to let them live, and the leaders of the assembly ratified it by oath.

JOSHUA 9:14-15

This passage reveals a fatal mistake made by the children of Israel. Joshua and his people were doing very well, and all the neighboring countries were frightened of them because of their victories and the power they had from the Lord.

Their neighbors, the Gibeonites, decided to trick Joshua into a peace treaty. So they made themselves look tired and dirty, like they had traveled a long way, and came to Joshua asking for a treaty. Here was a business transaction facing the Israelites. The men of Israel looked at the outward evidence, decided it looked like a good deal to them, and signed the bottom line.

They later found out they had been deceived. The facts were not as they appeared to be, and the Israelites had made a strategic mistake. Why? Because they trusted in their eyes and their minds, and did not inquire of the Lord.

There are times we think we don't need to consult the Lord; it's a cut and dried situation, in our view. So we make decisions in our own strength, based on our human reasoning, and that gets us in trouble.

Proverbs 3:5-6 tells us, "Trust in the Lord with all your

heart and *lean not on your own understanding;* in all your ways acknowledge him, and he will make your paths straight." Leaning on our own understanding is the norm, especially in the business world. But, as Christians, we should take all our decisions to the Lord and ask for his wisdom. Sometimes our own understanding is very shortsighted and incomplete. We need the eternal wisdom of our Savior; we need to inquire of the Lord.

Today's Challenge

To remember to inquire of the Lord in any decision I face, and not to lean solely on my own understanding. That can get me into trouble.

Today's Prayer

Lord, please keep me from arrogantly forging ahead on my own without inquiring of you today. Help me to remember that in every decision, every situation, I need your help and wisdom. I don't want to make the mistake of running on my own strength.

— ∾ —

Loving Others Like I Love Myself

"Teacher, which is the greatest commandment in the Law?"
Jesus replied, "Love the Lord your God with all your heart and
with all your soul and with all your mind.' This is the first and
greatest commandment. And the second is like it: 'Love your
neighbor as yourself.'"

MATTHEW 22:36-39

Jesus told us that the second-greatest commandment is that we should love our neighbor as we love ourselves. Like me, you've probably heard that all your life. But have you ever stopped to think about the consequences of putting it into practice?

I was meditating on this and thinking, "How can I ever get to the place where I truly love other people the way I love me?" I thought, "Well, how do I love myself?" That's pretty easy to answer. I love myself by taking care of all my needs. I try to provide all the comforts I can for myself. If I'm hurting, I try to find relief. If I'm hungry, I get myself some food. If I'm tired, I find rest. I know that I love me by the way I treat myself.

Then I asked myself, "What if you loved yourself the way you love others?" Turning that question around gives some additional perspective. If I treated myself the way I treat others, I think I would frequently feel deprived, and my feelings might be hurt. I would probably feel somewhat neglected if I loved myself the way I love others.

Love, then, is displayed in actions. We have to keep reminding ourselves that God's kind of love is not a gushy feeling, but it is rather a decision to act in loving ways. Therefore, it is possible for us to love others as we love ourselves if we treat others the way we treat ourselves.

One way we can learn to love others is to ask ourselves frequently, "If I treated myself the way I'm treating him or her, how would I feel?" For example, when you find yourself impatient with a co-worker who made a dumb mistake, stop and remember how tolerant and understanding you are with yourself when you do something stupid. Then, just simply remind yourself that you should treat that co-worker just like you'd treat yourself.

Today's Challenge

To love others in the way that I love myself.

Today's Prayer

Lord, I realize how well I treat myself and that is evidence that I love myself. Help me to treat others well because they are loved by you. Teach me how to love others in the same ways that I love myself.

FIFTY-FIVE

Live Independently; Depend on God

Make it your ambition to lead a quiet life, to mind your own business and to work with your hands, just as we told you, so that your daily life may win the respect of outsiders and so that you will not be dependent on anybody.

1 THESSALONIANS 4:11-12

We've heard a great deal about how our welfare system, instead of helping people as it was intended to do, has in many cases created a dependency on the government. There's fairly good evidence that this dependency is detrimental both to the individuals who receive the assistance as well as to our society as a whole.

We admire people who take care of themselves and help others. As Christians, we gain the respect of those outside our faith community to the extent that we take care of those who truly need help, and with our daily lives seek to be role models of this biblical principle of independent living.

Do you ever find yourself thinking that someone owes you something? That you deserve help or assistance or benefits, whether from the government, or from your boss or company, or from life in general? This attitude of entitlement leads to a kind of dependency, too. We all need to recommit ourselves to living independently, as Paul admonished us in this passage.

At the same time, we must cultivate another kind of dependency: a total dependence on the Lord. The same Apostle

Paul wrote to the Corinthians about the hardships he was suffering, and he said: "We were under great pressure, far beyond our ability to endure, so that we despaired even of life…. But this happened that we might not rely on ourselves but on God, who raises the dead" (2 Cor 1:8-9). To the men of Athens he said, "In him [God] we live and move and have our being" (Acts 17:28).

We are totally dependent on God for every breath we take, every talent and ability we have, every good and perfect gift that comes from above. We cannot operate independently of him, no matter how we try.

Today's Challenge

To live independently and not rely on others to do for me what I can and should do for myself. To depend totally on God in every area of my life.

Today's Prayer

Lord, help me today to be independent when it comes to doing my work and taking care of myself. Also help me to continually realize that I am totally dependent on you for guidance, love, peace, and life itself.

— ∼ —

Faithless Panic

When Jesus heard this, he was astonished and said to those following him, "I tell you the truth, I have not found anyone in Israel with such great faith."

MATTHEW 8:10

There are two interesting stories recorded in Matthew 8. The first is the story of the centurion, who asked Jesus to heal his servant simply by speaking a word of healing. The centurion had faith to believe that Jesus did not even have to come with him, though his servant was miles away. When Jesus heard this, he said, "I have not found anyone in Israel with such great faith."

A short time later, the disciples came to Jesus in a panic. Jesus was asleep in the boat, and a squall came up and quickly threatened to overturn the boat and to drown them all. They fearfully begged Jesus to do something. Jesus said to them, "You of little faith, why are you so afraid?" (Mt 8:26).

Notice that the centurion was commended for his faith, while the disciples were confronted for their lack of faith. Both needed help. Both sought help from Jesus. Jesus responded to both requests. But one was a faith-filled request and one was a faithless cry of panic.

The centurion expected Jesus to heal his servant—and believed he could do it long-distance. When Jesus calmed the storm, Matthew tells us, "The men were amazed and asked,

'What kind of man is this? Even the winds and the waves obey him!'" (Mt 8:27). They had come to him in panic, and yet were amazed that he could meet their need.

The centurion knew Jesus only by reputation. The disciples had spent much time with him. Yet the centurion showed great faith. He came with his need, but he brought expectation along with the need. The disciples came with their need, but they thought this storm was too much for Jesus.

Jesus invites us to come with our needs, too. The next time you're in a panic and need Jesus' deliverance, come with faith, believing that he will hear and answer.

Today's Challenge

To take every emergency situation to Jesus with complete faith in his ability to resolve the problem in his way and in his time.

Today's Prayer

Lord, I know that you invite me to bring all my burdens and cares to you, big and small. I want to learn how to turn to you when panic starts to build. Please increase my faith so that I can trust you no matter what crisis I face.

— ∼ —

FIFTY-SEVEN

Fishing for Solutions

When he [Jesus] had finished speaking, he said to Simon, "Put out into deep water, and let down the nets for a catch."

LUKE 5:4

When Jesus told Peter how to fish, I would imagine that Peter must have thought, "You're a carpenter, not a fisherman; what do you know about fishing?" But he soon learned that Jesus could be trusted to help him in his chosen profession.

In Luke 5 we read how Peter had fished all night and caught nothing; he was ready to give up and go home. But Jesus told him not to give up, but to go into deep water and put down his nets. You'll notice that Peter didn't go to him for fishing advice, because he'd never thought of the Lord as an expert on fishing.

No, instead Jesus intervened in this business dilemma without being asked. And he gave Peter some strange instructions. Peter knew that you don't fish in midday, you fish at night. And you don't catch fish in the deep waters.

Reading between the lines a bit, I wonder if Peter was not thinking, "Lord, it's not going to do any good. I appreciate your concern, but you just don't understand fish. However, I'll give you a lesson in fishing, and since you asked me, I'll go through this futile exercise and take the boat out, though of course it's just a waste of time."

So weary Peter, having worked futilely all night, obeyed the

Lord, probably with a martyr's complex. And, of course, he learned a great lesson: Jesus controls the fish, too. Peter broke all the fishing rules ... and he almost broke his nets because he caught so many fish.

Don't you and I do the same thing? We exclude Jesus and his authority from certain areas. After all, what does Jesus know about my difficulty at work? How could he help me with my job, or co-worker, or manager? So we go on in our own strength, "fishing all night," working hard, and finding few if any solutions, answers, or success.

Jesus has authority, power, and knowledge of all things, and if we allow him to guide us in all areas, we will discover, like Peter, that he knows what he's talking about. His methods are often unorthodox. Our faith will be tested. But then, how else would we know who was in control?

Today's Challenge
To turn to the Lord for wisdom and help in every situation of my life.

Today's Prayer
Lord, as the Creator of the universe, you are an expert at everything and everyone. Therefore, I ask for your wisdom and guidance in every area of my life today.

— ∼ —

Do Everything Without Complaining

Don't grumble against each other, brothers, or you will be judged.

JAMES 5:9

Here's a principle to apply in our daily lives: Never complain or grumble about each other. In 1 Peter 4:9 we read that we are to offer hospitality to one another without grumbling.

I remember once getting roped into doing something at church. It wasn't what I wanted, but somehow there I was, serving others. All the while, I was grumbling and complaining in my spirit about having to, and God showed me clearly that he wouldn't put up with that kind of attitude from me.

Philippians 2:14 says we are to do everything without complaining or arguing. But listen to the great benefits of practicing this biblical principle: "so that you may become blameless and pure, children of God without fault in a crooked and depraved generation, in which you shine like stars in the universe as you hold out the word of life." We will shine like stars and show others Jesus in us as we learn to do everything without complaining.

So, when you have a complaint, first of all, take it to the Lord. Just tell him how you feel and ask him for his perspective. You're going to be amazed at how your attitude will change. Then stop yourself when you hear those complaining words start to come out of your mouth. Just refuse to say them. Swallow them right then, in midsentence if necessary.

What a great testimony Christians would have, especially in the marketplace, if we truly practiced this principle. I challenge you to join me in learning to do all things without grumbling or complaining.

Today's Challenge

Not to grumble about any person or situation, and to serve others without grumbling.

Today's Prayer

Lord, it's so easy to get caught up in the grumbling and complaining that goes on around me each day. Please help me to swallow those words of complaint today, so that I can be a light to the people around me.

FIFTY-NINE

— ❧ —

Just Laugh!

A cheerful heart is good medicine, but a crushed spirit dries up the bones.

PROVERBS 17:22

Several companies have undertaken to make the work environment more fun, and have discovered it also makes employees more productive. Southwest Airlines hires people for their sense of humor and trains for skills; they are number six in the top ten of "America's Most Admired Companies" in *Fortune* magazine. Ben and Jerry's began their company with the intention of "having fun while making ice cream."

Laughter is cheap medicine. Sustained laughter stimulates an increased release of endorphins, the body's own natural painkiller. Endorphins actually diminish physical and psychological pain and stimulate the body's immune system. I'm told that twenty seconds of laughter is the equivalent of three minutes of strenuous exercise.

I notice when I go to my office totally work-focused, preoccupied with my schedule, I can cause a cloud of heaviness to hover over my entire staff. But when I share a funny story, laugh at myself, and "lighten up," it changes the atmosphere almost instantly.

God gave us laughter and humor as a wonderful antidote for our troubles. If you've been humor-impaired lately, why don't you ask God to help you laugh more today. It will help a lot.

Today's Challenge

To find more humor in my everyday routine.

Today's Prayer

Lord, help me to laugh more today. Teach me to see the humor, even in situations that are difficult. Keep me from being too heavy today. Give me a light heart that is filled with joy and laughter.

SIXTY

— ∾ —

Three Ways to Witness on the Job

I am not ashamed of the gospel, because it is the power of God
for the salvation of everyone who believes: first for the Jew, then
for the Gentile.

ROMANS 1:16

Does witnessing on the job scare you to death? Many Christians have the idea that witnessing means carrying large Bibles to work every day, or cornering people in the lunch-room and ramming the Four Spiritual Laws down their throats.

Let me suggest three things that all of us can do on our jobs that can be a positive witness for Christ.

First, be joyful. Most people you work with don't have much joy in their lives. Life is a struggle for them. You hear lots of complaining, and negative attitudes are everywhere. If you enter that scene with real joy in your life, it is the most powerful witness you can have.

A second way we can all witness, no matter what kind of situation we're in, is to do quality work. The Bible tells us to do with all our hearts what our hands have found to do. We will be held accountable to the Lord for the work we do for our employer. We have a much higher manager to report to than do our nonbelieving co-workers. A willingness to go the extra mile should be a trademark of a Christian in the working world.

The third thing we can all do is to pray. Pray earnestly for the people you deal with on your job—co-workers, managers, customers. Pray for them by name. Ask God to intervene in the problem relationships in your workplace. Pray for those in authority, that they'll do their jobs with integrity and efficiency.

Don't forget that people need the Lord. When you know Jesus, you hold the answer to the problems and struggles of everyone you know. With joy and gladness, come out from under cover as an ambassador for Jesus Christ and say with your life and your words, "I belong to Jesus; I'm not ashamed of the gospel."

Today's Challenge

To be joyful, do quality work, and pray for the people with and for whom I work.

Today's Prayer

Lord, remind me today that I am an ambassador for Jesus Christ. Help me to keep my joy throughout the day, to do my work to the best of my ability, and to pray for those in my work world.

SIXTY-ONE

— ❧ —

Are You Facing a Tough Decision?

*Am I now trying to win the approval of men, or of God? Or
am I trying to please men? If I were still trying to please men,
I would not be a servant of Christ.*

GALATIANS 1:10

A friend told me of the guilt trip she went through when she
and her husband decided that she would not go back to work
after her baby was born. She heard comments like, "Don't you
realize that you're ruining future opportunities for other
women in this company?" "Why are you giving up a position
you worked so hard to get?" "The company has invested all
this time and money in you, and you're simply quitting?"

Sometimes our priorities are not appreciated in the business
world, are they? This is when we have to ask ourselves the question Paul posed to the Galatians: "Who am I trying to please:
people or God?"

Of course, the hard part isn't asking ourselves the question.
The hard part is being honest with ourselves about that answer.
If you're like me, you like to please people because you like
their approval and acceptance. But sometimes we just can't do
both, and we have to choose. We can't serve two masters, Jesus
told us. That goes for all areas of our lives.

If you're facing a priority decision that could be misunder-
stood or criticized by others, I urge you not to be swayed by
others' opinions. Seek first to win God's approval, and then rest

in the assurance that pleasing God is far more important than pleasing people.

Today's Challenge
To be much more concerned with pleasing God than with pleasing people.

Today's Prayer
Lord, my human nature makes me prone to being a people-pleaser. Show me areas of my life where I am tempted to put other people's opinions ahead of my desire to please you. Please give me the desire and the courage to choose your way, regardless of how others react.

— ❦ —

SIXTY-TWO

Time Wasters—Interruptions

Therefore be careful how you walk, not as unwise men, but as wise, making the most of your time, because the days are evil.

EPHESIANS 5:15-16, NASB

Time is money! says the old cliché. But in actuality, time is more precious than money because, once you spend it, you can never replace it.

None of us can claim discrimination or unjust treatment on how time has been distributed. We all have exactly the same amount of time to spend each day: twenty-four hours—no more, no less. And God will hold us accountable for our use of time.

Do you have any idea where your time goes, or of the little things you do that waste time? One of our most common time wasters is interruptions. Every time we stop and start anything we're working on, we lose time and concentration. So when we start again, it takes us awhile to get back mentally to where we were before the interruption. Therefore, anything we can do to minimize our interruptions will save us time.

Think about who interrupts you most frequently. On your job it may be your boss, co-workers, or employees, asking questions or giving information. Ask yourself what would reduce the number of interruptions from those persons. Perhaps if you took time to do some training in some area, they wouldn't have to ask you so many questions. Maybe if some information were available in a written format, they wouldn't need to talk to you so often. Could you nicely suggest a set time to get together, on a regular basis if necessary, to cover everything at one time?

You might be surprised to discover how much time you can save, and how much stress you can reduce, by eliminating some of those unnecessary interruptions.

Today's Challenge
To eliminate as many interruptions as possible so that I can make better use of my time.

Today's Prayer
Lord, I realize that you entrust the resource of time to me, and I want to be a good steward of my time. Please reveal to me ways I can reduce the interruptions in my day so that I can work more efficiently.

SIXTY-THREE

—❧—

Truth About Self-Esteem

What a wretched man I am! Who will rescue me from this body of death?

ROMANS 7:24

When you read that statement by the apostle Paul, you might conclude that his self-esteem was very poor. How could he call himself a "wretched man"? Furthermore, in that same chapter he says he can't do the good he wants to do, and he does the bad he doesn't want to do. In today's terminology, Paul is suffering from low self-esteem.

Low self-esteem is the natural result of taking a look at our own sinful natures. Indeed, we need to first learn that, by ourselves, we have no lasting, secure basis for good self-esteem. People who are determined to have good self-esteem are doomed to spend the rest of their lives fighting to do and be and acquire and impress, so that they can feel good about themselves. And believe me, it's a losing battle, because you can never do or be or have enough.

This pursuit of self-esteem is impacted by your past, your circumstances, your failures, your abilities, your good breaks— by many things over which you have no control.

But wait, here comes the good news. Because of Jesus you and I can feel very good about ourselves when we bask in the truth that we have been made righteous in God's eyes through the death, burial, and resurrection of our Lord Jesus Christ.

Instead of trying to improve your self-esteem, pursue knowing God. As you do, you'll discover that feeling good about who you are in Christ becomes a by-product of knowing him. You'll begin to be used by God in the lives of others, and that will make you feel really good. You'll see how God increases your gifts and abilities as you work for him, and you'll feel good about that.

Today's Challenge

To refocus my pursuit of self-esteem and instead pursue knowing God and loving Jesus.

Today's Prayer

Lord, I sometimes get too involved in trying to feel good about me. Help me to realize that I can only feel good about myself when I am living my life in Christ and he is living his life in me. Deliver me from this dead-end pursuit of good self-esteem and instead help me to pursue you more.

SIXTY-FOUR

—— ∾ ——

Learning to Listen

A word aptly spoken is like apples of gold in settings of silver.
PROVERBS 25:11

Learning to listen before we talk is one of the smartest things we can ever do. We can save ourselves a lot of time and embarrassment, and clear up many misunderstandings before they start. Talking without listening, on the other hand, can bring shame not only to us, but also to our testimony for Jesus.

Here are a few ideas to become a better listener. First, don't think about what you're going to say while the other person is talking. Have you ever witnessed a conversation where nobody's listening? Each person waits for just enough silence to say what they're thinking. Good listeners discipline themselves not to think of their next sentence, but of what the other person is saying.

Don't interrupt or complete another person's sentences. That's an irritating habit. You may need reminders to help you break this pattern, so ask the people close to you to call it to your attention when you interrupt them or complete their sentences.

Paraphrasing is a wonderful listening and communication device. When you say, "Now, if I understand you correctly ..." and proceed to tell the other person what you heard him or her say in your own words, that person not only knows that you're listening, but also that you care enough to make sure you have heard correctly.

As Christians in the working world, we can distinguish ourselves by showing that we care through becoming better listeners. I encourage you to try, even if it takes a little effort. In the book of James we read: "Be quick to listen [and] slow to speak" (1:19). It's a good motto to put in front of you each day.

Today's Challenge

To show others that we care about them by becoming a better listener.

Today's Prayer

Lord, help me today to listen better. Remind me when my bad listening habits take over, and show me how to truly listen to others with a caring heart.

SIXTY-FIVE

— ∾ —

Can You Overlook a Fault?

A man's discretion makes him slow to anger, and it is his glory to overlook a transgression.

PROVERBS 19:11, NASB

Have you been provoked recently by something someone did or said to you? I know I have. A careless comment, an abrupt E-mail message, something taken from your work station without permission. If you choose, by God's grace, to overlook the transgression, it will be for you a glory—an admirable thing, a beautiful thing.

As I think back, I realize that there have been times when I could have—and should have—overlooked something that had been done to me. My anger may have been justifiable, but in some situations it would have been better just to let it go without demanding my day in court. I'd rather have the glory than the opportunity to ventilate my anger.

Remember, anger dissipates with time; what makes you very angry right this minute may look quite different in two hours. Also, anger is much stronger when we are tired or when our bodies aren't in such good condition. That's why we must be very *slow* to anger.

Psalm 145:8 says, "The Lord is gracious and compassionate, slow to anger and rich in love." Pray that verse into your life, asking God to make you gracious, compassionate, slow to anger, and rich in love. Then when you feel angry, you'll have the wisdom to know whether to overlook it or to express your feelings, and when and how. Don't let uncontrolled anger ruin your relationship with God or with the people in your life. It is possible to be victorious—to be angry and sin not.

Today's Challenge

To be patient and loving with those who annoy us; to repay thoughtlessness with kindness.

Today's Prayer

Lord, I'm sure there are many times when you have been "slow to anger" with me. May I reflect your patient loving kindness to those around me, especially those who deserve it least.

— ⁓ —

Paying Attention to What We Know

I am the Lord your God, who teaches you what is best for you, who directs you in the way you should go. If only you had paid attention to my commands, your peace would have been like a river, your righteousness like the waves of the sea.

ISAIAH 48:17-18

After reading this passage, I am reminded that anxiety and unrest result when I don't pay attention to and put into practice what I already know about God. Rarely do I need to know some new truth or principle; I just need to practice what I teach other people.

I think that's true for most of us. We've been taught and given clear guidelines, but our feet tend to stray. Our commitment to follow what we know needs daily refreshing.

"If only you had paid attention ..." Isaiah wrote. It's rarely a deliberate decision on our part to wander from God's principles. More often we simply fail to pay attention. Our focus gets fractured, our center shifts slightly, and a little side step gets us off track. What results is loss of peace, loss of blessings, loss of fellowship.

If you are feeling anxious, restless, or out of sorts today, check it out. Have you failed to pay attention to God's will for you? Have you failed to practice daily what you already know?

Jesus said, "If you know these things, you are blessed when you do them." Knowing and doing are two different things.

Simply knowing doesn't bring rest or peace. Doing does. If we will pay attention to the commands of our Lord, both large and small, we will know "peace like a river and righteousness like the waves of the sea."

Today's Challenge

To pay attention to where I have stopped doing what I know I should do. To take inventory of where I have inadvertently let my guard down.

Today's Prayer

Lord, help me to pay attention to the truths and principles that I already know. Reveal to me any area where I've wandered away from what you have already taught me.

— ❧ —

"Zero-Budgeting" Our Lives to Fit God's Plans

"I have brought you glory on earth by completing the work you gave me to do."

JOHN 17:4

In business and in government we hear the term "zero-budgeting," a budgeting process that starts each year at zero. Everything in the budget is up for scrutiny and reconsideration; each budget item must be justified. For example, if you had a budget last year for travel, you may or may not have it next year. Before the money will be approved, you must demonstrate a need for it.

At the end of his ministry, Jesus was able to say that he had completed the work the Father gave him to do. That's because his agenda was always the Father's agenda. Time and again he said, "I do what the Father tells me to do."

For us to be able to finish the work God has for us, we need to start at point zero and say, "Lord, what would you have me do?" We also need to ask ourselves some penetrating questions, such as:

- Is there anything I have said that I would never do? Is that my agenda, or God's?

- Are there any areas in my life where I keep saying, "Hands off—don't touch this, God"?

- What assumptions do I have about what God wants me to do, or not to do? Are those assumptions from God, or are they my own?

Zero-budgeting may lead us to make some radical changes, or it may confirm for us that we're to stay where we are, doing what we're doing. But when we give God permission to set the agenda, we can have tremendous peace and freedom, and we can say with Jesus, "I have brought you glory on earth by completing the work you gave me to do."

Today's Challenge

To be willing to do zero-budgeting in my relationship with the Lord, and to give him permission to make changes in my life wherever he pleases.

Today's Prayer

Lord, I want you to know that I truly desire to do the work you have given me to do, not to run my own agenda. Please show me where I need to do some zero-budgeting in my life, and give me the strength to truly turn all controls over to you.

SIXTY-EIGHT

— ∾ —

Bones in the Desert

Yet in spite of all these wonderful experiences many of [our ancestors] failed to please God, and left their bones in the desert. Now in these events our ancestors stand as examples to us, warning us not to crave after evil things as they did.

1 CORINTHIANS 10:5-6, PHILLIPS

When Moses led the children of Israel out of Egypt, he had no way of knowing that thousands of them would never make it to the Promised Land of milk and honey. Though they all had experienced God's miraculous deliverance time and again, many of them left their bones in the desert.

Why? Paul tells us it's because they set their hearts on evil things. "They sat down to eat and drink and got up to indulge in pagan revelry" (verse 7). They were totally self-centered, seeking above everything else to satisfy their physical, emotional, and social needs!

We see the same thing all around us today. I can think of many people who in times past walked with God, and experienced blessings and miracles in their lives. But today they're doing their own thing, walking away from God, never entering God's Promised Land for them.

We'll never find fulfillment in the desert that this world offers. Rebellion against God's principles is one sure way to guarantee that life will be dry, sun-parched, fruitless, and boring. I know the neon lights are bright, but they are empty promises, leading you into a desert where you'll simply deposit your bones in a fruitless search.

To be fulfilled, to move into that Promised Land of peace and love and security that you want, you have to go God's way. Jesus said, "Blessed are those who hunger and thirst for righteousness, for they shall be filled" (Mt 5:6).

Today's Challenge

To avoid being deceived by the allurement of the world and thinking that it has anything of value to offer.

Today's Prayer

Lord, please keep me from deception today, as I mingle in this world where you have placed me. May my eyes be open to see the real truth of the world's deceptions, so that I don't wander in a dry land and end up just depositing my bones in that desert, with nothing of eternal value to show for it.

— ∽ —

Are You A Demanding Supervisor?

Each one should use whatever gift he has received to serve others, faithfully administering God's grace in its various forms.

1 PETER 4:10

A young supervisor, who had several men working under him, wrote me of his particular dilemma. In his position he finds it hard to strike a balance between leading his men and serving them. He wants to be a servant, but he also must get the job done. This young man felt that in some situations he had to do things as a supervisor that seemed harsh and un-Christlike.

Any Christian in a management position has felt this dilemma. How can we get the job done, demand good work, and still have a servant's heart to administer God's grace?

Think of Jesus and his staff of twelve men. Do you think he was demanding of their time? I get the feeling that those men put in many long, hard days. I know that Jesus had high expectations of them, and often expressed his disappointment when they failed to live up to his expectations. Yet there's no doubt that he showed them great love and concern, giving freely of himself to teach them and help them grow.

Being a firm supervisor, and ensuring that the employees who work for you do their jobs right and put in a good day's work, is not contrary to Christian principles of love and kindness. Of course, we cannot ask of others what we do not give ourselves. Jesus never asked more of his disciples, in terms of time and hard work, than he was willing to give.

As long as your people see you putting in an honest day's work, you have earned the right to expect the same of them. Quite frankly, you will be doing your employees or co-workers a favor to teach them the rightness and the blessing of hard work, honesty, and diligence.

Today's Challenge

To set a high standard of excellence for work done by those I work with or who work for me, without becoming an unreasonable taskmaster.

Today's Prayer

Lord, help me to model excellent work today, and teach me how to lovingly require it of others who look to me for leadership.

— ❧ —

Dealing With Difficult People

All the people in the synagogue were furious.... They got up, drove him out of the town, and took him to the brow of the hill on which the town was built, in order to throw him down the cliff. But he walked right through the crowd and went on his way.

LUKE 4:28-30

Jesus' hometown crowd was so angry at him for claiming to be who he was that they wanted to kill him. Jesus knew there was no reasoning with this angry mob, and he knew when to walk away.

There were other situations where Jesus dealt with difficult people very directly. When the Pharisees and religious leaders got on their high horses and made false accusations against Jesus, he was often extremely direct in telling them to "cool it." But I notice that Jesus was never out of control when he confronted those people. He knew exactly what he wanted to say, said it with emphasis, and did it to teach and help others.

We can learn a great deal from Jesus about how to handle unreasonable, difficult people. Sometimes we need to walk away instead of trying to have the last word or convince another person that he or she is wrong. There are people who will never be won by reason or facts, and if we insist on showing them the error of their ways, we will make the situation worse.

There are times when we must take a stand and be willing to confront. However, our motivation in a direct confrontation should be carefully scrutinized to be sure we do it for the good of the other person, and that we are not attacking the other person out of malice or a sense of vengeance. In confronting an angry or difficult person, we should be certain that we do it under the Holy Spirit's control.

Today's Challenge

To be very discerning in resolving confrontational situations.

Today's Prayer

Lord, in my work world I sometimes encounter unreasonable and difficult people. I want to deal with them as you would, so please give me the discernment and wisdom I need to know the best way to approach them. Please also give me the patience I need to follow through.

— ❧ —

SEVENTY-ONE

A Servant Attitude

Jesus knew that the Father had put all things under his power, and that he had come from God and was returning to God; so he got up from the meal, took off his outer clothing, and wrapped a towel around his waist. After that, he poured water into a basin and began to wash his disciples' feet, drying them with the towel that was wrapped around him.

JOHN 13:3-5

Washing feet was the lowest of servant's jobs, a humiliating task. And yet, Jesus took it upon himself to wash the feet of his disciples because of the power of God in his life. He even washed the feet of Judas, the man who he knew was going to betray him within a few hours. Amazing!

Now, the last job the God-Man should have been doing is the lowly job of washing feet. But in doing so, Jesus taught us that spiritual power is demonstrated in service. Spiritual power does not lead us to a life of grandeur and recognition, of fame and luxury. It leads us to a life of serving others.

If you want to see a really spiritual person, look for someone who's always doing something for someone else, even the lowliest task. They may not have name-recognition status with the world, but they surely do with God.

The ability to be a servant comes as a result of God's power in us. We can't work it up in ourselves. Servanthood is not a natural desire; it has to come as a result of supernatural power.

The more we allow God to work his will in our lives, the more that power will be evidenced through acts of service.

To be willing to be a servant to others.

Lord, it is not my natural desire to serve others. Rather, I tend to want to be served. Help me to realize that when your power is at work in my life, then I will want to be a servant. Send someone my way today that I can serve in your name.

— ❧ —

A Question-Generating Life

When they saw the courage of Peter and John and realized that they were unschooled, ordinary men, they were astonished and they took note that these men had been with Jesus.

ACTS 4:13

We don't have the opportunity to preach a sermon on our job, nor would it be appropriate. We can't give the Four Spiritual Laws to a co-worker very frequently. But there's no question that our lives can preach a sermon every day, letting people around us know that we have been with Jesus.

In 1 Peter 3:15, we read that we are to be ready to give an answer for the hope that is in us. But before we can give answers, we must have someone ask the right questions.

Living a "question-generating" life is our challenge on the job. But when the questions are finally raised, it's our responsibility to be ready with an answer that is both clear and full of love and gentleness. No faltering, no hemming and hawing, no hesitation.

How? Well, each situation is different. We can say a lot to some people, while others allow us only a few sentences here and there. While it's true that some Christians witness insensitively and do some harm in that way, it is far more often the case that as Christians we don't use the opportunities we are given. We aren't prepared or willing to take our stand and give a strong witness.

Notice how Jesus witnessed to people. Often he just dropped a statement that left everyone curious. People were always asking, "What manner of man is this?" Jesus always got the attention of his audience. He knew how to get them to ask him questions.

That's our perfect model for witnessing. Live the Word of God in front of your co-workers daily. When you do, you'll eventually have an opportunity to answer questions put to you, and that's the best kind of verbal witness you can give.

Today's Challenge

To live a life that generates questions, and to be ready to give an explanation for the hope in me.

Today's Prayer

Lord, help me to live in such a way today that it creates questions in the minds of those around me who have not yet accepted your salvation. Please make me sensitive today to any questions that come my way that are open doors for a witness.

SEVENTY-THREE

— ◇ —

Are You Content?

I know what it is to be in need, and I know what it is to have plenty. I have learned the secret of being content in any and every situation, whether well fed or hungry, whether living in plenty or in want.

PHILIPPIANS 4:12

Someone once wrote: "The uncommon life is the product of the day lived in the uncommon way." A person whose life is exciting and full is one who finds meaning and satisfaction in the seemingly insignificant, daily things in our lives.

Let me give you a very simple example: I have some china that I really love. It gives me great pleasure to set my table with that china, to hold it, even to wash it. I remember once, when my daughter was very young, that she found it rather strange to hear me getting excited about this china that I had owned for years. I said to her, "If you can find pleasure and joy in the little things in your life, your life will be full of pleasure and joy. Otherwise, it's going to be very drab most of the time, with a few high points only now and then."

All of our lives are made up in large part of daily duties, mundane tasks, repetitive responsibilities. Nobody escapes them. Regardless of how green that grass looks in someone else's garden, believe me when I tell you that their lives are very "daily," too.

But no matter how humble and unremarkable your daily

life may seem, you can revel in it if you can learn to enjoy and appreciate the "dailyness" of your life—if you can appreciate what you have. As the apostle Paul tells us, the secret is learning to be content in any and every situation. It brings meaning to our daily lives, and frees us from the dreariness of looking over our fence at someone else's grass.

Today's Challenge

To learn to be content with who I am, where I am, and what I have.

Today's Prayer

Lord, help me learn to be content. It is not a lesson that comes easily for me. Deliver me from always looking over my fence and wishing my life were different in some way. Help me to appreciate all the good things in my life today, big and small.

SEVENTY-FOUR

— ∾ —

Are You an Undercover Christian?

Whoever acknowledges me before men, I will also acknowledge him before my Father in heaven. But whoever disowns me before men, I will disown him before my Father in heaven.

MATTHEW 10:32-33

For many years I was an undercover Christian. I didn't want to stick out in a crowd, be a fifth wheel, or look or act differently. Maybe you can relate.

Often we go undercover for one or more of these reasons:

- We don't want to be rejected by our work associates, or do damage to our career by holding too tightly to Christian ethical standards.

- The very idea of witnessing scares us to death because we don't know how.

- We're afraid of breaking a law or being "politically incorrect" if we mention the name of God in secular environments.

- Our lives don't measure up to Christian principles, and we're ashamed to say we're Christians.

Consider this: God has designed work as the common denominator for the Christian and non-Christian. This is no accident. Many of us would retreat into our sheltered worlds and avoid any contact with unbelievers if we weren't pushed into it because we have to work.

Jesus said he has sent us into the world. None of us is exempt from this. And a large part of your world is your workplace, whether that world is an office, a retail store, a hospital, a factory, or wherever. That is the world into which you are sent.

Does your world know that you are a representative of Jesus Christ, his ambassador? Does it know there is something different about you? Don't miss your opportunities today to be out in the open for the Lord. Remember, if you're ashamed of him, he will be ashamed of you.

Today's Challenge

To look for ways to "blow" my cover, to show that I am not ashamed to claim Jesus as my Savior.

Today's Prayer

Lord, help me not to be ashamed today to tell others what you have done for me. Give me wisdom and discernment in sharing my faith, but please show me how to proclaim my faith in you in positive and bold ways.

SEVENTY-FIVE

— ∾ —

Coming on God's Terms

"But when the king came in to see the guests, he noticed a man there who was not wearing wedding clothes. 'Friend,' he asked, 'how did you get in here without wedding clothes?' The man was speechless."

MATTHEW 22:11

The man in this parable came to a wedding dressed in his "Friday casuals," knowing full well that he was going to be underdressed. "After all," he undoubtedly thought, "what difference does it make? I know you're supposed to wear those fancy wedding clothes, but I'd rather be comfortable. I'm going to do it my way."

So he went to the wedding, and was confronted by the king for his improper dress. Notice that he was speechless—he had no excuse. He obviously knew better, but must have thought he could get by with it. Can't you hear him reasoning, "Surely the king won't throw me out just because I didn't wear the right clothes!" He seriously misjudged the king.

When Jesus told this parable, he said the king told the attendants, "Tie him hand and foot, and throw him outside, into the darkness, where there will be weeping and gnashing of teeth." You see, he had to come on the king's terms; there was no other way, no compromise. After all, it was the king's wedding, and he had the right to say what was proper and what wasn't.

Many people today want to come to God on their own terms, in their own way. They think: "Surely God wouldn't reject me just because I don't believe in Jesus." "I can't believe God would be so narrow-minded that there would be only one way to know him." "I can find God in my own way."

So they come on their terms, expecting God to compromise his standards for them, to change his word, to make an exception. But God never, never does that. He is immutable—he never changes, his principles never change.

If we come to God, it must be on his terms, not ours. To do anything else is to invite rejection. But the good news is that God's door is open always if we will come his way, and that's through Jesus Christ, and Jesus alone.

Today's Challenge

To avoid being deceived by the common philosophy that all roads lead to God. To be willing to come to God on his terms.

Today's Prayer

Lord, I gladly come to you through Jesus Christ, and confess that your way is not only the best way, it is the only way.

— ∾ —

A Strange Job Interview

When they had finished eating, Jesus said to Simon Peter,
"Simon son of John, do you truly love me more than these?"
"Yes, Lord," he said, "you know that I love you." Jesus said,
"Feed my lambs."

JOHN 21:15

Just before Jesus returned to heaven, he wanted to be certain that Peter was prepared and qualified for the job that was ahead of him. So Jesus asked Peter three key questions—a type of job interview, if you will. Here is what he asked:

1. Peter, do you truly love me?
2. Peter, do you truly love me?
3. Peter, do you truly love me?

That's a strange job interview, don't you agree? Notice that he didn't ask Peter about theology. He didn't ask him about his education or experience. Not once did he ask about Peter's awards or credentials, or question Peter about his gifts or abilities.

Yet the Lord was very careful to quiz Peter repeatedly about the most important prerequisite for service, the one essential ingredient Peter would need in order to serve the Lord faithfully and not give up easily. And that was simply: "Peter, do you truly love me?"

It's still the basic job interview question Jesus asks us today, if we desire to be his disciple. For when we truly love Jesus, everything else flows from that love.

If we truly love Jesus, we won't find it difficult to spend time with him. We'll rearrange our schedules to make time for him. We'll devour his Word, because it is the bread of life. That's the normal response from someone who really loves Jesus. He told us that if we love him, we will keep his commandments. Love produces obedience.

If Jesus were interviewing you today for a position as his disciple, how would you answer the question, "Do you truly love me?"

Today's Challenge

To search my heart and mind for a candid answer to the probing question: "Do you truly love me?"

Today's Prayer

Lord, I realize that loving you is the basic job requirement for being your follower, your disciple. I want to love you, Lord, more and more. Please show me how I can grow in my love for you so that I am qualified to "feed your sheep," and do your work.

— ∾ —

SEVENTY-SEVEN

Cookie-Cutter Christians

But godliness with contentment is great gain.

1 TIMOTHY 6:6

Are you content with the personality God gave you? Each of us is unique; God doesn't make cookie-cutter Christians. And our personalities are a key part of our identity. Some of us are "people" people, some are project people. Some of us are outgoing and gregarious. Others are reserved and quiet. Some are leaders; others are followers. There are many variations in the personalities God has given us.

Each personality has its strengths. For example, a gregarious, outgoing person makes friends easily and puts people at ease. But the quiet, reserved person is a very good listener who people turn to when they need a shoulder to cry on or an ear to listen. Because they are quiet, they rarely hurt people's feelings or cause confrontations. They are often peacemakers.

For many years I thought my take-charge, entrepreneurial personality was a mistake; it seemed to me that women shouldn't be like me. I even seriously tried one time during my college years to change my personality altogether and be like other people. I'm sure you know that I couldn't make that change happen. God gave me a particular kind of personality and I'm stuck with it!

However, in the last few years, I've come to really appreciate my personality, as unusual as it may be at times. I like the

161

way God has made me. I take great pleasure in "leading the way," breaking new ground, and taking risks.

There are some serious flaws that accompany my personality, of course. Rather than excuse those flaws with a glib, "Well, that's just the way I am!", I want to polish my personality so that the defects and problems that exist will gradually weaken and be eliminated altogether.

I can honestly say now that I like the way God created me. Can you?

Today's Challenge

To understand my personality strengths and appreciate the way God has made me, and to work on my personality weaknesses.

Today's Prayer

Lord, sometimes I can see the problems with my personality and get so focused on what's wrong with me that I fail to appreciate the good things about myself. I want to thank you for the wonders you have created in me, and ask you to help me be more content with who I am.

SEVENTY-EIGHT

— ≈ —

Dead-End Job: Preparation for the Future

*For the revelation awaits an appointed time; it speaks of the
end and will not prove false. Though it linger, wait for it; it
will certainly come and will not delay.*

HABAKKUK 2:3

God put David in the fields, taking care of sheep. In that most
unlikely place, God taught David some wonderful skills—one
of which was how to kill a lion and a bear. As a shepherd,
David had plenty of time to perfect his skill as a marksman. He
worked with that slingshot until he was an expert, in that
seemingly unimportant, going-no-place job of taking care of
dumb sheep!

I look back on my life and realize that in those quiet times
of my life, when it looked like nothing was happening, I was
learning skills and doing things that have equipped me to do
what God has for me to do now. God is efficient, and he
knows how to prepare us for the job ahead.

David didn't know, when he was tending sheep, that God
was preparing him to be king. He had no idea. But he did that
job well, and while he was doing it, God was quietly training
him for great things. His skill with a slingshot enabled him to
kill Goliath, which started a chain of events that eventually ele-
vated him to the throne. His future as king began in those
lonely fields, shooting stones from a slingshot day in and day
out.

If you're in the training fields right now, don't blow the opportunity to develop your own gifts. You never know what God has planned for you just around the corner.

Today's Challenge

To be patient in my job, realizing that God may be preparing me for something greater through my experience in this current job.

Today's Prayer

Lord, I know that I can trust your timing in my life, and I know that you never waste anything, so I believe that even in my present job you are working something out for my good. Though I can't see what that is now, I thank you for it, and ask for patience to wait for it.

SEVENTY-NINE

— ❦ —

Practicing the Fruit of the Spirit

But the fruit of the Spirit is love, joy, peace, patience, kindness, goodness, faithfulness, gentleness and self-control. Against such things there is no law.

GALATIANS 5:22-23

Many are concerned these days about the legal limits we face in sharing our faith, especially in the workplace. What is within the law and what isn't? Well, one thing's for sure, it is never against the law to demonstrate the fruit of the Spirit on your job.

Why not determine to strengthen your witness at work by focusing on a different fruit of the Spirit each week? Let's say this week you choose kindness. Each day you could pray specifically that God would give you a kind heart and a kind tongue toward the people you work with and for. Ask God to show you specific acts of kindness that you can do for others. The goal might be to do at least one kind thing for someone every day.

Then, all through your day you could look for these acts of kindness. Maybe your co-worker is swamped and stressed out with a heavy workload. You could offer to stay an extra hour and help him or her, or cover the phones for this person for a couple of hours, or something like that. Or perhaps someone has had car trouble. You could go out of your way to take this person home or give him or her a lift somewhere.

Keep in mind that these kind things must not be done in order to make others obligated to you in any way, but simply because you want to be kind and to establish better relationships with people. The next week, you should choose another fruit and think of ways to demonstrate that fruit on your job.

This will teach you a lot about the practical application of God's Word in your daily life, and it will open new doors between you and others.

Today's Challenge

To take seriously the living out of the fruit of the Spirit in my life.

Today's Prayer

Lord, it's easy to talk about the fruit of the Spirit, but I want to see these characteristics alive in my everyday life. Please give me the desire and the discipline to focus on developing this fruit in the way I interact with the people on my job.

EIGHTY

— ～ —

Dealing With Angry People

He who answers before listening—that is his folly and his shame.

PROVERBS 18:13

What do you do when you're confronted with an angry, irate person? There are some helpful steps to remember that will, in most cases, allow you to help that person calm down.

First, listen and allow that person to ventilate. Many times an angry person simply needs to "get it off his or her chest." Once that happens, he or she will often calm down.

Then, use gentle words to turn away the wrath. Once you begin to speak, your choice of words and your tone of voice become very important. Choose empathetic words, like "I can understand your frustration" or "I certainly can see why that would upset you." You can sympathize with an angry person without apologizing. Don't be afraid to use sympathy, such as, "I'm sorry you've had a problem" or "I'm sorry this has inconvenienced you." Combined with a sincere tone of voice, these are gentle answers that will turn away wrath.

Remember that no one is in your life by accident, even those difficult, angry people. God gives us these opportunities to demonstrate his love and his power to those people and to others who are watching us. Don't blow your opportunities. Learn to deal with angry people in a gentle and wise way.

Today's Challenge

To deal gently with angry people and help to defuse their anger.

Today's Prayer

Lord, help me remember to use gentle words today if I encounter anyone who is full of wrath or anger. Please keep me from reacting in an out-of-control way, and teach me how to respond with gentleness and compassion.

EIGHTY-ONE

God Doesn't Fight Battles Our Way

"For my thoughts are not your thoughts, neither are your ways my ways," declares the Lord.

ISAIAH 55:8

Have you noticed that usually God leads us to fight the giants in our lives in the most unusual ways? David was able to defeat a nine-foot giant with a simple slingshot. King Saul thought he should use armor and a sword, but David was gifted with a slingshot (see 1 Samuel 17).

Remember when Peter had fished the way fishermen are supposed to fish, and he had caught nothing? Finally when he did it the way Jesus said to, even though it broke all the rules of fishing, he caught so many fish that it almost sank his boat (see Luke 5).

When Jehoshaphat was facing a great army, destined to be defeated, he marched straight into battle, sending the singing men in advance to praise God for the victory. And when they got to the battlefield, the enemy had killed each other in confusion. That's not a normal military strategy, but God was leading Jehoshaphat, and Jehoshaphat was willing to do it God's way (see 2 Chronicles 20).

We have to learn to walk by faith and trust the Holy Spirit within us to give us guidance, and then not doubt it when others say, "That's not the way to do it," or "Nobody has ever done it that way before." God just doesn't work by our rules, but if we trust him, he can and will work miracles in our lives that we've never dreamed could happen.

Why does God work in these "mysterious ways"? To teach us to live by faith and not by sight. He is pleased when we trust him, and this teaches us to trust. Also, this way we won't take the glory for ourselves. If we could get it done our way, we might lose sight of his power and start to think we did it through our own efforts.

Today's Challenge

To trust God and his way in my life, even when I don't understand what he is doing.

Today's Prayer

Lord, I know that without faith it is impossible to please you, and I definitely want to please you. Therefore, I want to learn to trust you more and increase my faith. Please help me let go and trust your way in my life even when I don't see how it's going to work!

EIGHTY-TWO

— ❧ —

Leave Your Water Jar

Then, leaving her water jar, the woman went back to the town and said to the people, "Come, see a man who told me everything I ever did. Could this be the Christ?"

JOHN 4:28-29

The Samaritan woman who encountered Jesus at the well was there to get water. She came in the middle of the day when it was hot probably because she was an outcast, not accepted in polite society, and she didn't want to run into all the other women who got their water in the cooler morning hours. She brought with her the heavy water jar she always filled and carried home on her head.

But when Jesus offered her a never-ending supply of living water, she was so thrilled with her discovery that she left her water jar to rush back into town and tell everyone she could find about Jesus. This woman left behind with Jesus her burden—her weight. This was the toilsome task she had to perform daily, a humiliating, tiring, boring job; that water jar was a symbol of poverty because she had to get her own water.

That water jar is a symbol for us as well, a symbol of the burdens we carry around until we meet the Savior. When we discover our Source of living water, we realize that we no longer need our water jars. We can put them right at Jesus' feet, and go forth to tell others about him, free from the burden, free from the guilt, free from the humility of our past, free from our poverty and weariness, and alive unto Jesus.

What is your water jar today: Some past sin or failure? Some difficult job you must do? Some great disappointment? Why do you continue to carry that water jar and fill it up with earthly water, earthly solutions? Jesus is waiting at the well to give you living water; he is the answer to your need, and you can leave your water jar right at his feet and go forward, with freedom and lightness.

Today's Challenge

To leave my "heavy water jar"—the burden or heartache that weighs me down—at Jesus' feet today.

Today's Prayer

Lord, help me to drink deeply from your living water inside of me. Today I choose to lay my "water jar" _____ at your feet.

— ✑ —

Reduce Stress—Slow Down, Wait

Be still before the Lord and wait patiently for him.

PSALM 37:7

One of my greatest challenges is to relax and enjoy my life. I'm always in a hurry, even though often there is no need for me to hurry. Being still does not come easily for me.

Tell the truth, do you stand in front of your microwave oven and say, "Come on, hurry up"? Or do you complain that your FAX machine is too slow? Isn't it amazing that our new computer seems slow to us after a very short time? Nothing is fast enough for us these days. Our society is built on speed and instant gratification, and when we allow ourselves to get caught up in that mentality, we add much additional stress to our lives.

Actually, there is great joy in anticipating things and waiting for something for a time. When we get everything we want right away, we really miss out on a lot of joy. Thinking of what we want, dreaming about it, waiting for it—all of these can enhance our enjoyment of what we want when we do get it. But if we get caught up in the "I want it now" mindset, we miss the joy of anticipation and heap stress on ourselves.

David advises us to be still and wait patiently for the Lord. I'm certain he had to remind himself of that very often. He waited a long time before he was crowned king of Israel, even though the prophet had declared that God had chosen the shepherd boy as king. David had to learn to wait patiently for the Lord's timing in his life, and so do we.

Watch out for that old stressor, hurry and rush. Slow down; be still; wait patiently; relax. Your stress level will decrease and you'll enjoy your life so much more.

Today's Challenge

To avoid the pitfalls of the "I want it now" mentality and learn to relax and wait patiently.

Today's Prayer

Lord, it isn't easy for me to wait, and certainly not to wait patiently. Teach me the valuable lesson of how to be still, and the joy that comes when I wait patiently on you.

EIGHTY-FOUR

— ∾ —

Be Willing to Change

"I tell you the truth, unless you change and become like little children, you will never enter the kingdom of heaven."

MATTHEW 18:3

Change is required of all of us, every day. Yet we still resist it as though change in itself were bad. Certainly not all change is change for the good, but we can never improve without changing. Jesus warned us that unless we change our hearts and humble ourselves like little children, we will never enter the kingdom of heaven. Many people will miss heaven because they aren't willing to change.

What are the things in yourself that you keep intending or trying to change, but haven't yet? *You're going to be more organized; you're going to eat better; you're going to start exercising regularly; you're going to read your Bible and pray more.* Lots of us have good intentions for making changes in our lives, but too often those intentions are never realized.

One of the major reasons we resist change is because it is very uncomfortable. We have dug ourselves some little ruts in which we operate. Those ruts frequently are bad habits that need to be replaced, but we've been there so long that we're comfortable there. As soon as you start to change anything, you go into a transition period that is anything but comfortable.

But unless you're willing to stagnate where you are, you

have to learn how to incorporate change into your life in little and big ways. There are many skills, disciplines, and good habits that we can learn only by teaching ourselves to change.

I want to encourage you not to let the discomfort of change keep you from it. Expect it to be uncomfortable. It won't last forever, but it will be there awhile. Live through the uncomfortable feelings, but don't give up.

Today's Challenge

To be willing to change where change is needed, and to live through the uncomfortable transition period that change always entails.

Today's Prayer

Lord, help me to be willing to change. I want to be humble and teachable so that I can become more and more like Jesus. Show me where I need to change and give me the grace and ability to make that change happen.

— ❧ —

Possessed by Our Possessions

"Do not store up for yourselves treasures on earth, where moth and rust destroy, and where thieves break in and steal."

MATTHEW 6:19

How easy it is for us to be possessed by our possessions. In fact, many of us heap tons of unnecessary stress on ourselves because we place far too much value on the things we possess.

A woman I know couldn't enjoy her own grandchildren because of her expensive antiques. She was a nervous wreck when her grandchildren came to see her, for fear they might damage her valuable possessions. Then this woman learned that she had cancer, and suddenly she realized how confused her priorities were. Grandchildren were infinitely more important than antiques, and so she got rid of most of her valuables and stopped worrying about the rest of them.

Another friend and I were having lunch together when she accidentally spilled something on her silk blouse. Like any of us, she fretted about the damage, wondering if the stain would come out, worrying about the cost of having it cleaned. I sympathized with her, because I've been there so often myself. But I reminded her that it was just a blouse, and we laughed together.

Is there anything you own that owns you? Have you ever noticed that the more expensive something is, the more stress you'll feel if you lose it or it breaks? We pay a price when we invest so much in our things that we have to worry about them. My rule of thumb has become that when something I own causes me more stress than the enjoyment it is supposed to bring, it's time to get rid of it.

Maybe you've been accumulating too much stuff, trying to get the best of everything, and you've never stopped to think that you are possessed by your possessions. Why don't you get rid of some things today, and begin to reduce your stress?

Today's Challenge

To examine my attitude toward my possessions and see if something I own really owns me.

Today's Prayer

Lord, I know that my life does not consist of possessions, but sometimes I still get caught in the treasures trap. Please help me to enjoy all you've given me, but never to hold possessions so dear that they become sources of stress.

EIGHTY-SIX

— ∾ —

Limping Along

So tighten your loosening grip and steady your wavering stand.
Don't wander away from the path but forge steadily onward.
On the right path the limping foot recovers strength and does
not collapse.

HEBREWS 12:12-13, PHILLIPS

Are you limping along today, spiritually speaking? Does it seem like God is far away, that your prayer time is unrewarding and dead? Does your mind wander when you read the Bible, and do the words run together on the page? Does it seem like a dry history book rather than a love letter to you from the Lord? Has your desire to be involved in ministry grown cold, and are you going through the motions out of a sense of duty?

If so, well, you've got a spiritual limp. We all get them, and we need to be prepared to deal with them. Most of us want to leave the race when we start limping, don't we? We figure we just can't keep going, so we give up and sit on the sidelines or start down another path that looks a little easier. But that's not the way to deal with a spiritual limp.

Tightening your grip and staying on the right path, regardless of how you feel or whether you are getting results, require discipline. The first verse of that twelfth chapter of Hebrews tells us we must run with endurance the race marked out for us. We may even run the race with a limp, but we must not sit down or get sidetracked.

Let me encourage you today to keep running in the right race, even though you're limping along. If you'll keep doing what you know you should do, even without feelings or results, your limping foot will recover, and pretty soon you'll be running strong again.

Today's Challenge

To avoid the natural tendency to quit when there is a "limp" in my spiritual walk with God.

Today's Prayer

Lord, teach me the very important principle of not giving in to my emotions when there is a "limp" in my walk. Help me to stay on the right path until I find healing.

EIGHTY-SEVEN

— ∾ —

Open Doors With Creativity

Though I am free and belong to no man, I make myself a slave to everyone, to win as many as possible…. To the weak I became weak, to win the weak. I have become all things to all men so that by all possible means I might save some. I do all this for the sake of the gospel, that I may share in its blessings.

1 CORINTHIANS 9:19, 22-23

The apostle Paul was as creative as he could be in order to reach as many as possible with the gospel. He eliminated barriers between himself and others—artificial barriers that made communication difficult. And in that way, he had opportunities to share the gospel with many people who otherwise would never have listened.

A friend of mine found herself in a difficult work environment with some people who were prejudiced toward her and had built artificial walls based on their prejudices. Instead of pouting or throwing a pity party for herself, she started "Project Love." She wrote up some creative lunch invitations, and each week she invited one of her co-workers to lunch as her guest.

When presented with these unusual invitations, her co-workers found it difficult to say no. Week after week she "did lunch," until she had covered all her co-workers. As a result, they began to get to know her as the wonderful person she is. In fact, the woman who was most prejudiced against her became a close confidante and depended on her for counsel and help many times.

Project Love was a creative door-opener. Yes, it required a bit of risk-taking on my friend's part, but she was willing to take that risk. She was willing to make the first move toward people who had not treated her with a great deal of kindness. And it worked!

Today's Challenge

To find a way to break down barriers that exist between me and my co-workers so that I can have an opportunity to show them the love of Christ.

Today's Prayer

Lord, I recognize that there are some artificial barriers between me and others at work. Please help me to find creative ways to break down those barriers so that I can show them your love.

EIGHTY-EIGHT

— ❧ —

The Power of "I'm Sorry"

If we confess our sins, he is faithful and just and will forgive us our sins and purify us from all unrighteousness.

1 JOHN 1:9

A good friend of mine told me recently that the biggest difference between her and her non-Christian co-workers is that she apologizes a lot more than they do! She struggles with things in her life, just like you and I do. But she is willing to say, "I'm sorry," and God is changing her day by day. I'm convinced her apologies are witnesses to the power of Jesus.

Have you recently lost your temper with a co-worker, told a lie to your manager, or deceived a customer in some way? If so, your conscience probably hasn't stopped bothering you, and that's good. When our own sin doesn't bother us, we are in a very dangerous position. A prickling conscience is God's way of prompting you to take advantage of his offer to forgive you and purify you; all you have to do is confess.

Maybe you're wondering how you could ever be a witness for Jesus, since you know you've failed and others know you've failed, and what's more, you may fail again. But everybody struggles with failure, and those who are not Christians have no good way to deal with the guilt that often accompanies failure. One of the best ways to witness is to own up to our own failures, make restitution where necessary, and share that God is a forgiving and restoring God.

Obviously it is better *not* to fail, but isn't it great that God uses even our shortcomings? Don't let some failure or fear of failure keep you from being a bold witness for Jesus. Remember, he can turn your ashes into beauty, if you will let him.

Today's Challenge

To recognize that even my failures can be an avenue of blessing and witness for the Lord.

Today's Prayer

Lord, I've often been hamstrung by my fear of failure and the knowledge of my past failures. Please help me to understand that you specialize in taking even my blunders and turning them into instruments of praise.

EIGHTY-NINE

— ∾ —

Breaking Sin's Stranglehold

"If your hand causes you to sin, cut it off. It is better for you to enter life maimed than with two hands to go into hell, where the fire never goes out."

MARK 9:43

This is one of the most startling statements Jesus ever made. Imagine the disciples' response. Cut off a hand? Pluck out an eye? What was Jesus thinking? But Jesus was using strong language deliberately; he knew both the power of sin and the painful consequences of playing around with it.

The message is clear: regardless of what it takes to be free from the control of any sin in our lives, we should take that drastic action, because it would be better to enter life maimed or crippled than to be controlled by some sin.

I once answered a letter from a single woman who said that her boyfriend, who was supposedly a Christian, was urging her to have premarital sex. She asked for my advice on how to deal with him. I advised her to break off the relationship and never to see him again. I can imagine that she found that counsel to be very drastic; if she did follow my advice, it was no doubt somewhat painful for her. But far better that she remain single, even for the rest of her life, than to continue to see a man who would encourage her to sin.

Is your job or place of employment causing you to sin? Then you need to resign and find a new job. Do you have a friend who is influencing you to do what you know is wrong? It's time to end that friendship. Perhaps you are reading or watching things that cause you to sin. Burn the books or magazines; throw your television away; stop going to movies.

Do whatever it takes to break the power of sin in your life. No compromising; no negotiating; no halfway measures. Cut out the cancer. Remember: You can choose your sin but you can't choose its consequences.

Today's Challenge

To be ruthless about any known areas of sin in my life.

Today's Prayer

Lord, please forgive me for playing around with the sin of _____. I confess it to you, and ask you to deliver me. Help me to take whatever drastic action is necessary to break the power of this sin in my life.

NINETY

— ∿ —

Lift Up Your Hands!

I will praise you as long as I live, and in your name I will lift up my hands.

PSALM 63:4

Have you ever noticed how many times Scripture describes hands being used to worship God?

- *Clap your hands, all you nations; shout to God with cries of joy.* PSALM 47:1

- *Lift up your hands in the sanctuary and praise the Lord.* PSALM 134:2

- *I want men everywhere to lift up holy hands in prayer.* 1 TIMOTHY 2:8

Why should hands play such an important role in worship?

Think of how a baby or young child lifts up his or her hands to mom or dad, looking at that parent with total devotion and dependence. Those uplifted hands touch your heart, don't they? You can't resist them because they're saying to you, "I need you; I love you."

Don't you think that God wants to see that attitude from us, his children, when we come to worship and praise him? Uplifted hands are a universal sign of devotion and dependence, and I find that lifting my hands in worship really helps me to remember how much I need the Lord, how dependent I am on him.

It is also a humbling thing to lift up your hands. It is an admission that you're not capable on your own. So, by lifting our hands in praise and worship, we are glorifying the Lord, and by lifting our hands in prayer we are acknowledging his lordship.

Today's Challenge

To recognize my total dependence upon the Lord, and to offer him my work today as a "sacrifice of praise."

Today's Prayer

Lord, I lift my hands to you to tell you I love you, I need you, and I'm not ashamed to declare my faith in you.

NINETY-ONE

— ❧ —

How to Show Love and Concern for Workers

Do nothing out of selfish ambition or vain conceit, but in humility consider others better than yourselves. Each of you should look not only to your own interests, but also to the interests of others.

PHILIPPIANS 2:3-4

As Christians we should be concerned about the personal welfare and feelings of the people who work for and with us. Yet it can be challenging to find a way to care for people's personal needs and still get our jobs done. How can we show a loving and caring attitude toward those in our work worlds?

The first thing we can and should do is to pray regularly for all our co-workers, especially those who report to us. Pray for them specifically by name. As much as you can, learn something of their personal situation so that you can pray for them effectively. Pray for their job performance and their relationships and attitudes on the job as well. That's the best thing you can do for them.

Remember that your attitude toward these people will clearly indicate that you care about them. Treat them with respect; ask them about themselves; give them recognition when they deserve it; make allowances for personal situations when you can; treat everyone with fairness and honesty—all of these are ways to show God's love to your co-workers and to serve them.

As Christians in the marketplace we have unique opportunities to demonstrate what Jesus is like by the way we care about others. If you truly care about other people, loving them as you love yourself, placing their welfare above your own, you can be certain they'll know it.

Today's Challenge
To find ways of showing love and concern for my co-workers.

Today's Prayer
Lord, in the midst of my busy days, I can easily forget to show concern for those in my work environment. Please give me the desire and the wisdom to be a loving, concerned person while at the same time getting my job done.

— ∾ —

What Is Caesar's, and What Is God's?

Then he [Jesus] said to them, "Give to Caesar what is Caesar's, and to God what is God's."

MATTHEW 22:21

Think of "Caesar" as your employer. What are you required to give to your "Caesar"? Here are a few important obligations a Christian has to an employer:

1. *Hard work.* We must be careful to apply ourselves conscientiously and work our full shift. Christians should never take advantage of employers by cheating them out of time or work that is due to them.

2. *Protection of the employer's assets.* Those pencils and pens, paper clips and pads supplied by your employer are not for your personal supply room at home. The telephone is another costly asset that we can abuse in the way we use it. Expense accounts should be meticulously honest and fair.

3. *Loyalty.* As an employee, you represent your employer outside the workplace. This means that, while you are taking money from that employer, you owe them respect. Don't complain about them or run them down to others. Your loyalty reflects well on the company ... and on you.

On the other hand, there are certain things that you do you *not* owe your employer. For example, you are never obligated to participate in activities that bring dishonor to God.

You do not owe your employer anything that would affect your personal integrity, including "little white lies." Nor do you owe your employer all of your time, energy, or talent.

When an employer requires any of these things from you, it's probably time to look for another job. Never render to Caesar the things that belong to God.

Today's Challenge

To draw a clear line between what I owe my employer and what I owe God, and never to compromise those standards.

Today's Prayer

Lord, I want to do a better job of giving what I honestly owe to my employer without compromising my commitment to you. Please teach me how to do that, and give me the strength to follow through.

— ❧ —

NINETY-THREE

Handling Insults

That is why, for Christ's sake, I delight in weaknesses, in insults, in hardships, in persecutions, in difficulties. For when I am weak, then I am strong.

2 CORINTHIANS 12:10

When I read this verse, I want to say to the Apostle Paul, "Who are you kidding? You want me to believe that you delight in all these bad things? I can believe you endure them, but to delight in them seems like an impossibility, Paul."

I remember receiving a very pointed insult—in writing, no less. When I read it, I can assure you I didn't say, "Oh, I delight in this insult." No, it made me angry, because it was unfair, as well as potentially harmful.

But as I pondered this verse and my situation, I realized that I really should be delighted. You see, I'd been feeling very good about my performance as a business trainer, and subtly I was becoming very self-confident, maybe even a little cocky, and I didn't even realize it! So God graciously allowed me to receive an insult—timed just right, to show me this problem before it got out of hand.

I can honestly tell you that I was finally able to rejoice in that insult. Not at first, but as I saw it through God's eyes, then I was able to thank him for showing me again—really rather painlessly—that it's only when I'm weak that I am strong. It's only when I recognize my need for him that his power can operate in me.

So, if some insult comes your way today, don't forget that you can rejoice in it if you look beyond the insult to find out what God wants to teach you through it.

Today's Challenge

To learn how to deal with insults that come my way, even to delight in them when I realize that they help me to find my strength in God alone.

Today's Prayer

Lord, thank you for the power of your Spirit in me. Because of that power, you can teach me how to rejoice in any insult that may come my way. Thank you that when I understand my human weakness, then I am truly strong.

NINETY-FOUR

God-Confidence, Not Self-Confidence

Now as they observed the confidence of Peter and John, and understood that they were uneducated and untrained men, they were marveling, and began to recognize them as having been with Jesus.

ACTS 4:13, NASB

When I think of a very self-confident person, I think of the apostle Peter. He was the only disciple who was confident he could walk on water. He was confident in his fishing abilities and knowledge. He was confident that Jesus was wrong to say he was going to die, and rebuked him for it. He was totally confident that he, Peter, would never deny Jesus, even if everyone else did, even if he had to die with Jesus.

However, all that self-confidence failed him at critical moments. He started sinking after taking a couple of steps on water. Self-confidence didn't keep him up. Self-confidence didn't fill his empty nets with fish after a long night of fishing. Only when he followed Jesus' instructions was he able to catch fish. Though he was very confident in rebuking Jesus, Jesus not only refused his counsel, but considered it to be satanically inspired. And within hours of his most confident assertion that he would never deny Jesus, he did so three times with cursing and swearing.

Thank God, however, that's not the end of Peter's story. We see a transformed Peter in the book of Acts. He was still extremely confident, still assertive, still a leader, but the results were very different. For Peter had lost all his self-confidence, but gained in its place God-confidence. Notice that the loss of self-confidence didn't turn Peter into a wimp. He was more bold than ever before, because his confidence was in someone much more capable and powerful than himself—the Holy Spirit.

Today's Challenge
To operate in God-confidence, not self-confidence.

Today's Prayer
Lord, sometimes I buy into this world's message that I have to be full of self-confidence. Today help me to remember that I need to place all my trust in you, not in myself, and that when I do, you will give me boldness, courage, and confidence to do everything you have for me to do.

— ∼ —

NINETY-FIVE

Fretting About the Uncontrollable

A fool gives full vent to his anger, but a wise man keeps himself under control.

PROVERBS 29:11

Don't you think we often spend a lot of time and energy fretting about things that are beyond our control? Solomon reminds us that a wise man keeps himself under control, and in order to do that, we have to stop trying to control the uncontrollable.

For sure there are many, many things in life that are not controllable: the weather, the economy, the company's decision to "down-size," the drunk driver who hit your car—the list goes on and on. So, what do we typically do when we encounter the uncontrollable people and things in our lives?

Frequently we try to change them, only to discover we don't have the power to do so, and we end up even more frustrated. Another way some people deal with the uncontrollable is to live in denial and to pretend the problems don't exist. Many people try the runaway method: they move around a lot, change jobs frequently, can never find a church they like, and are always on the run.

Whatever method we use in trying to control the uncontrollable, we always end up frustrated and disappointed, and we do ourselves great harm as we build up anger and bitterness. We get vindictive and vengeful, and we add immense stress to our lives!

Remember this proverb today, and let go of the "uncontrollables" in your life. Focus instead on controlling yourself, and when you do, you'll have the wisdom and patience you need to cope with those uncontrollable things and people.

Today's Challenge

To recognize the uncontrollable people and situations in my life, and let go of them.

Today's Prayer

Lord, so often I waste time and energy trying to change people and things beyond my control. Help me to entrust those things to you today, and to focus my energy on controlling myself.

NINETY-SIX

Watch Out for Wrong Relationships

You say, "We want to be like the nations, like the peoples of the world, who serve wood and stone." But what you have in mind will never happen.

EZEKIEL 20:32

The children of Israel are good examples of how wrong relationships can be harmful. God told them that they must not associate with the idolatrous people of the other nations. And yet, that's just what they did. Time and again, God's children would try to make friends with idolaters, and every time they got into trouble. They surrounded themselves with the wrong people and little by little, they decided they wanted to be like their friends and associates.

The people around us, the people close to us, the people we listen to and try to please have enormous impact and influence in our lives. If they're the wrong people, our walk with God will suffer.

Now, Jesus set us an example of being a friend to sinners. We should be as well. But at the same time, we must carefully guard ourselves against relationships that cause us to compromise or lower our standards.

Ask yourself: Do my relationships enhance my walk with God? Are there people I voluntarily spend significant time with who are influencing me to deny, compromise, or walk away from my commitment to Jesus Christ?

Proverbs 4:23 reminds us: "Above all else, guard your heart, for it is the wellspring of life." Your heart here refers to your mind, your attitudes, your opinions, and your motivations. This includes everyone that influences your heart and mind. Guard it well, because it is the wellspring of your life—the source and supply of everything that happens in your life.

Today's Challenge

To survey all of my close relationships and determine if I am allowing someone to have a bad influence in my life.

Today's Prayer

Lord, give me insight to see if I am being poorly influenced by anyone in my life. Help me to choose relationships that enhance and encourage my walk with you.

— ∾ —

NINETY-SEVEN

Pray for Those in Authority

I urge, then, first of all, that requests, prayers, intercession and thanksgiving be made for everyone—for kings and all those in authority, that we may live peaceful and quiet lives in all godliness and holiness.

1 TIMOTHY 2:1-2

We are to pray for peaceful relationships with those in authority. If you're dealing with an incompetent or unfair boss, have you been praying for him or her regularly? Until you begin to truly pray for this person, you won't see much change in your attitude or in his or her behavior.

Smart employees understand that their job description includes making their boss look good. The world uses that principle as a manipulative tool, but we have other reasons for doing it. First Corinthians 13 describes the kind of love we are to develop in our lives, a love that is like God's love. That kind of love "does not delight in evil but rejoices with the truth. It always protects, always trusts, always hopes, always perseveres" (1 Cor 13:6-7).

As Christians we are to ever be seeking to have God's love fill us and overflow through us to everyone in our lives, including our incompetent bosses. Therefore, we should try to make them look good because God's love motivates us to protect others from bad exposure, to delight in the good things they do, not the bad things, to try to smooth over their mistakes whenever we can honestly do so.

Can you begin today, by faith, to ask God to give you his love for your boss? Are you willing to allow God to give you the desire and the wisdom to want to make your boss look good, to promote his or her welfare? If you will take just that first step toward God in this direction, you're going to discover that he will pour his grace into your life and enable you to do what now looks impossible.

Today's Challenge
To pray for my boss, and to do everything I can to make him or her look good.

Today's Prayer
Lord, thank you for my boss. Please show me ways I can make him or her look good; help me to avoid any negative talk that goes on about him or her. Give me the desire to respond to _____ in the right way.

NINETY-EIGHT

— ∼ —

Giving Up the Control to the Lord

Stand still and see this great thing the Lord is about to do before your eyes!

1 SAMUEL 12:16

This is probably the most difficult command in the Bible for me. I want to say, "Come on, Lord; why 'stand still'? Why not 'Get busy and do this and that and then you'll see the great thing the Lord is about to do before your eyes'?" That would be so much easier for me.

I don't like standing still. I love movement. I love busyness. I love activity. I love to-do lists. *Let's go; let's do; let's make things happen. You can do it. Just keep trying. Keep on keepin' on.* Those words are music to my ears, but not *stand still.*

It's hard for me to stand still because I'm a controller. I want to be in charge. I'd rather drive than be a passenger; I'd rather give a presentation than listen to one; I'd rather lead than follow. So I constantly struggle to take control of any situation I'm in. Therefore, "stand still and see this great thing the Lord is about to do before your eyes" is hard for me to do.

At one point in my life I was going through a particularly difficult period of "standing still." As I would start trying to take the controls back in my own hands, I would hear the quiet voice of God in my mind saying to me, quite simply, "Can't you trust me?"

That's what it takes to stand still—it takes trust. And when

203

you and I are willing to take our hands off, give up the control, and stand still, we are saying to Jesus, "I trust you. You're smarter than I am. You can run this show better than I can." When we stand still and demonstrate our faith in him, he is pleased, and he can do a great thing for us.

Today's Challenge

To stand still and give up the controls of my situation, my life, to God.

Today's Prayer

Lord, I realize how much I try to control everything, instead of standing still and letting you have the lead in my life. Please help me to trust you more so that I can see the great thing you are going to do for me instead of messing everything up by trying to control it myself.

— ∽ —

NINETY-NINE

Lazy Hands

Lazy hands make a man poor, but diligent hands bring wealth.

Sometimes we tend to think that it takes special gifts or talents to be successful in life, but do you know what really makes someone successful? It's about 90 percent hard, diligent work. It is never giving up; it is going on when you feel like quitting; it is more perspiration than it is inspiration.

People often tell me that they would love to do what I do. I'm sure that some parts of my ministry look rather glamorous and exciting. But let me assure you that is only the tip of the iceberg. Beneath the surface are many hours of diligent work, staying at the job, and working hard.

I sit at my computer for hours, trying to come up with new ideas, doing the research, finding the right words, and getting it on paper—it is not glamorous. There is no handwriting on my walls; I often write pages and pages that eventually are discarded because they're not good enough. It is hard mental work most of the time.

In Proverbs 12:24 Solomon again tells us that "diligent hands will rule, but laziness ends in slave labor." If you want to be the one in charge, you need to be prepared to work very hard. True, there are some who have gotten to the top without earning it, but those are exceptions to the rule. More often than not, the person who rises to any level of authority is the one who has diligent hands. Lazy people typically end up at the bottom of the ladder. Your ladder to success begins with diligent hands, right where you are.

Today's Challenge

To work with diligence and avoid being lazy.

Today's Prayer

Lord, I want to have diligent hands today. Please remind me to work hard all day long and do the best I can do. Please keep me from being lazy and slothful.

ONE HUNDRED

—◇—

Settling For Second Best

"For I know the plans I have for you," declares the Lord, "plans to prosper you and not to harm you, plans to give you hope and a future."

JEREMIAH 29:11

Settling for second best is a common occurrence. People settle for second best in their marriages, in their jobs, in their goals and objectives, in themselves. God's plans are always the best for us. Why do we settle for less?

One main reason we settle for second best in our lives is because we are impatient. This has always been one of my major problems, but I'm learning how good it is to wait for God's first best in my life. When God puts us in a waiting room, we'll shortchange ourselves and have to live with second best if we refuse to wait for His guidance and direction.

Another reason we settle for second best is that we're not willing to be committed to discipline and hard work. We'd love God's best handed to us on a silver platter, but our motivation sags when extra effort is needed. Sometimes it's just sheer laziness that keeps people from having first best in their lives.

A third reason we settle for second best is that we don't really trust God. Many times we're actually frightened that God will do something we won't like or ask something of us we don't want to do. So, instead of getting his first best for our lives, we settle for second best.

How do I know? I did it for ten years—determined to fill my vacant place with what I thought would make me happy. But everything I tried was inferior—vastly inferior to God's first best for me.

God's first best is worth waiting for. It's worth your total commitment, and every ounce of your trust. God's first best will always be something more wonderful than anything you could cook up on your own.

Today's Challenge
To refuse to settle for God's second best in my life.

Today's Prayer
Lord, so often I am willing to settle for something less than your best for me because I'm impatient or lazy or greedy. Please keep me from this trap today and help me to hold out for your best in my life.

ONE HUNDRED ONE

— ∾ —

Weeping With Those Who Weep

Rejoice with those who rejoice; mourn with those who mourn.

ROMANS 12:15

Have you ever felt awkward when trying to help someone who is going through a difficult time? I find that sometimes my tendency is to avoid people who are hurting because I don't know what to say to them. This proverb gives us some good advice on how to reach out to them.

I remember quite a few years ago when my best friend's mother died. She called me at my office to tell me. It was not unexpected, as her mom had been struggling with terminal cancer for quite a few years, but even so it was a shock. When Fran called, the first thing I heard on the phone was, "Mary ..." and then she couldn't say anything else.

My response was, "Oh, Fran, Mom's dead, isn't she? I'm so sorry." And we both wept on the phone. Later she told me that it had been so comforting to her to talk to me, because I wept with her. She said others had, with good intentions, tried to comfort her by reminding her that her mother was much better off because she was relieved of her pain. But that didn't comfort her as much as someone crying with her.

When people are hurting, they just need to hear us hurt with them. Proverbs 25:20 says, "Like one who takes away a garment on a cold day, or like vinegar poured on soda, is one who sings songs to a heavy heart." You know what happens when you pour vinegar on soda? It fizzes and bubbles and is quite agitated. It is not a calming, soothing reaction.

Heavy-hearted people don't need trite sayings. They don't need to be reminded of what they know. They need someone to listen; to let them talk about their grief and pain. They need someone who doesn't try to find easy answers, but just cares enough to cry with them.

Today's Challenge

To be sensitive to anyone in my pathway today who is hurting, and to be willing to hurt with them, without lectures or clichés.

Today's Prayer

Lord, help me to see the people around me today who need someone to hurt with them, to cry with them. Give me compassion and love to reach out to them in your name.

ONE HUNDRED TWO

— ∼ —

Watch Out for Hand-Made Idols

Their land is full of idols; they bow down to the work of their hands, to what their fingers have made.

ISAIAH 2:8

In the Old Testament, many times the prophets spoke out against idols that were made with the hands. We tend to think those passages are not relevant to our lives today because we don't bow down to idols. Yet, there are many ways in which we worship what our hands have made. For example, many people worship their own success. They sacrifice much on the altar of getting ahead and attaining power.

Of course, there's nothing wrong with success unless we put it above every other concern. There's nothing wrong with making money unless money becomes our highest priority. I know many single people who want to be married more than they want anything else; even marriage can become an idol. An idol is anything we worship; an idol is whatever is more important to us than anything or anyone else.

God reminds me of areas in my life that can easily consume me. Working and doing can become idols for me. I often pray that God will deliver me from being addicted to busyness. The approval and commendation of others can become an idol for me.

Idols are not limited to the heathens or nonbelievers of our day. Even children of God can be tempted to worship at the altars of our own hands. But God doesn't like idols made with our hands any more than he liked those wooden and gold and silver idols made by his people in Old Testament times.

Today's Challenge

To be on guard for any hand-made idols that may take over my life.

Today's Prayer

Lord, help me to remember that I am susceptible to idol worship, just as were people of old. Show me those areas in my life where I tend to worship the work of my hands, and please deliver me from this idol worship.

—◇—

A Working Covenant

It pleased Darius to appoint ... three administrators over them, one of whom was Daniel.... so that the king might not suffer loss.

DANIEL 6:1-2

Daniel's job was to see that the king did not suffer loss; he performed his duties so well that no one could find fault with his performance.

Daniel's example is a good model for us to follow as well. As soon as we agree to do work for someone for certain wages, we enter into a covenant with that person or organization. True, it may be an unwritten covenant, but it is real nonetheless.

Because we are committing ourselves to the success of the organization for which we work, it's important that we work for organizations that are above reproach and worthwhile. A woman once talked with me about her job in a video store that rented soft porn videos. She was trying to justify her decision to take that job, since she didn't personally watch or approve of pornography. I advised her that she was helping her company make a profit from pornography. How could any Christian justify that activity?

Assuming you are working for a reputable, good organization that performs worthwhile services and makes good products, are you doing everything you can to keep your employer from suffering loss? Christians should see that as their highest priority on their jobs—to work hard for the people who pay them.

Daniel was in very difficult circumstances, in a foreign land against his will, away from his support system at home. But none of that changed his commitment to do what was right. He rose to the top of his organization because he was so good at his job. Whether or not we climb the ladder, our reputation should be solid when it comes to our work ethic.

Today's Challenge
To do everything I can to make my employer successful.

Today's Prayer
Lord, help me to remember my duty to be a loyal and hard-working employee, and to make my company successful. Show me how to work more effectively, not to climb the success ladder, but to bring honor to you, as Daniel did.

— ∼ —

When Others Are Jealous of You

Now when Daniel learned that the decree had been published, he went home to his upstairs room where the windows opened toward Jerusalem. Three times a day he got down on his knees and prayed, giving thanks to his God, just as he had done before.

DANIEL 6:10

Daniel gives us a wonderful example of how a Christian should handle jealousy. His peers were maliciously trying to destroy him because they were jealous of his position and power. So they cunningly had an edict established prohibiting people from praying to any god except the king, and the penalty was the lion's den. You know the rest of the story.

Frankly, had I been in Daniel's shoes, on hearing about my co-workers' evil plan I think I would have gone right to the king. I would have defended myself and tried to protect myself from the harm planned against me. I would have tried to get those co-workers into some hot water of their own, and probably would have felt justified in doing so.

Daniel didn't resort to vengeance, however. He simply continued to live his life, perform his job as always, and honor God without compromise.

Is someone plotting against you out of jealousy, trying to do you harm in some way? Be careful how you respond. Notice that Daniel prayed as soon as he learned of his coworkers' evil plan. That should always be step one. Ask God for wisdom and patience. Affirm to God that the most important outcome in the situation is that his name be glorified, not that you be exonerated.

Then let God fight the battle for you. Each situation is different, so there's no one right plan of action, but the principle here is that we never operate from vengeance or anger or personal retribution. Instead, allow God to show you how he can be honored through the situation.

Today's Challenge

To concentrate on what I have to do, rather than worry about those who may be trying to do me harm.

Today's Prayer

Lord, when people try to do me harm, I often react with vengeance and anger. Please help me to let go of these battles and do what you want me to do, allowing you to handle those who would do me harm.

Learning to Be Patient

Be patient, then, brothers, until the Lord's coming. See how the farmer waits for the land to yield its valuable crop and how patient he is for the autumn and spring rains. You too, be patient and stand firm....

JAMES 5:7-8

To say that patience does not come easily for me is an understatement. For the past few years I've been praying a lot about being patient, and believe it or not, I am more patient today than I used to be.

Here are some little secrets that are helping me to learn how to be patient. When you are emotional about any situation, it is not the time to act. Stand still until your emotions have calmed down and you can be certain that you're thinking straight. Often we really want to do something when we're upset or angry, because our emotions are at such a high. But whatever you do or say at that moment will usually be wrong. So wait to respond until your emotions are under control.

I've learned to discipline myself to sleep on it rather than to respond immediately when I am in an upsetting situation. Whatever it is that you think you have to do or say, get at least one good night's sleep before you do it. How different things can look the next day!

One woman told me that when she's upset, she writes down whatever is bothering her on a piece of paper and puts it aside for two days. After two days she takes it out and decides if it's still important. If so, she does something. If not, she tears up the note and puts the problem behind her. That's a good discipline to help you learn to be patient.

In a world that screams to us, "Don't just stand there; do something," God's voice often whispers to us: "Don't do something; just stand there." Or, as James puts it, "Be patient and stand firm."

Today's Challenge
To learn how to wait for God's timing in all I do.

Today's Prayer
Lord, I want to be a patient person because that is an evidence of your Spirit working in my life. By your Holy Spirit help me learn how to be patient. Teach me to resist the temptation to act in haste out of emotion, and instead to wait patiently for you.

— ∾ —

Learning to Ignore

Ignoring what they said, Jesus told the synagogue ruler, "Don't be afraid; just believe."

MARK 5:36

Do you know when to ignore what other people are telling you? We know it's important for us to be good listeners, but the opposite side of that truth is that there are times we should absolutely ignore what other people are saying to us.

The synagogue ruler in Mark 5 had asked Jesus to come and heal his sick daughter. On the way to his house some of his friends met them and reported that his daughter was dead, so there was no need to bother Jesus anymore. In response to those words of death and doom, Jesus told Jairus to believe and not be afraid, and he completely ignored the friends' bad report.

When he got to the house and announced that the child was not dead, everyone laughed at him. But Jesus ignored that too. He went in and brought the girl to her feet, alive and well.

It seems there are always people around to give us negative, discouraging words. They may be well-intentioned; they may be your best friends. But if their words of advice are faith-destroying words, then you should ignore them.

What are faith-destroying words? Anything that causes you to lose faith in the Lord, to doubt that he will answer your prayer, to wonder if his promises are really true, to question the validity of God's Word.

Jairus had to choose to believe Jesus in spite of what his friends said to him, even when they laughed at him. Undoubtedly he had some knots in his stomach as they walked to his house; he may have even felt a little foolish, but he chose to believe the words of Jesus. And those words were life-giving.

Today's Challenge

To learn to ignore others when they give me faith-destroying words and advice.

Today's Prayer

Lord, please give me the discernment to know when I should ignore words and advice from others. Help me to put my trust in you and not to allow the faith-destroying words of others to have any effect on my faith.

— ∾ —

Deborah—A Different Kind of Woman

Deborah, a prophetess, the wife of Lappidoth, was leading Israel at that time.

JUDGES **4:4**

Deborah's leadership and accomplishments would be outstanding today. In her day they had to be incredible. She was one of the judges of Israel, the top authority in the country. She had men working for her; she even led the army into a battle and won it. That certainly was not a customary role for women in her time.

She must have felt like a fifth wheel at times. She was different from all the other women in her day! It must have been a lonely spot. Undoubtedly there were times when she grew weary of the responsibilities and pressures on her. But she was a woman of great faith in God, and her dedication to her calling was unwavering, whatever personal desires she may have had to forego.

We know that she was married; we don't know if she had any children. But this was a woman in a traditional role, yet called by God to a job that was very untraditional. She had a position of higher authority than her husband—than any other man in the country. And yet Deborah was a judge because God called her to be one. God had gifted her for the job and that was his plan for her. God is sovereign and he uses many different kinds of people in different situations as he sees fit.

Today God still calls some women to do things not often done by women. He has a right to do so now, just as he did with Deborah. But the women God calls are not marching for women's rights. They are marching in the Lord's army, followers of Jesus Christ, committed to his service, regardless of the role they are asked to fill.

If God has called you to an unusual role, count it a privilege.

Today's Challenge

To never allow man-made prohibitions to prevent me from doing God's will.

Today's Prayer

Lord, I give you permission to use me in any way you want. I will be glad to follow traditional paths or to break new ground. I just want to know that you are leading me.

— ❧ —

Yoked Together With Unbelievers

Do not be yoked together with unbelievers. For what do right-eousness and wickedness have in common? Or what fellowship can light have with darkness? What harmony is there between Christ and Belial? What does a believer have in common with an unbeliever? What agreement is there between the temple of God and idols? For we are the temple of the living God.

2 CORINTHIANS 6:14-16

This is a biblical principle which gives us very clear guidelines concerning partnerships. Certainly the most important partnership decision anyone faces is their lifetime marriage partner. It is extremely important that we never even consider marrying someone who is not a believer. If we ignore this principle, we will not have the close, intimate marriage we desire.

Business partnerships would also come under this principle from 2 Corinthians. When you have a legal or implied partnership with someone in business, that fits the definition of being "yoked together." So, if you are a believer, it is clear that any business partner you choose should also be a believer, sharing your Christian principles and business ethics.

You may be wondering if this applies to an employer, or to our co-workers. Should a Christian work for a person who is not a Christian, or with people who are not Christians? Should Christians work in an organization that is not managed by Christians? An employee is not a partner in a business, so therefore I don't believe this applies in these situations. Being "yoked together" would apply where there is some legal or financial bond between two people.

However, we do need to be selective about the organization for which we work. We certainly don't want to expend our daily efforts for any company that is not producing a worthwhile product or service.

So if you're in business with someone, or contemplating it, remember that if you choose the wrong partner, you will be inviting disaster into your business endeavor as well as your spiritual life.

Today's Challenge

To make certain I do not choose to be in partnership with those who are not believers.

Today's Prayer

Lord, I know we are in this world but not of it. Help me to remember that it is wrong to be in a partnership with someone who is not yet in the family of God. Please give me wisdom and courage so that I am not yoked together in any way with unbelievers.

— ∾ —

A Heavy Workload

Do not be anxious about anything, but in everything, by prayer and petition, with thanksgiving, present your requests to God.

PHILIPPIANS 4:6

Do you have more to do than you can get done today? Are a lot of people making unreasonable demands of you? Is your head spinning with a myriad of details to be attended to, calls to be made, fires to be put out?

Whenever I feel pulled in too many different directions, I grow anxious and worry begins to raise its ugly head. Worry buys us nothing but more trouble. Has worry ever solved a problem? Has worry ever helped you think clearly and make good decisions? Has worry ever lowered your blood pressure?

There is a difference between worries and concerns. A worry is something you cannot affect through any action on your part. A concern is something that requires action and calls for a response. When we worry, we waste valuable time and energy on issues over which we have no control. The worry simply makes it more difficult for us to cope.

If you will release your anxiety about your workload and responsibilities to God right now, present your concerns to him in prayer, request what you need from him, and recite what you have to be thankful for, you will discover that you can face this day one step at a time. Do what you can, promise only what you know you can deliver, and leave the rest in God's hands.

Today's Challenge

Not to worry about all that I have to do. Every time worry starts to enter my mind, I will deliberately turn it over to God.

Today's Prayer

Lord, here is what I'm worrying about: (recite each worry in as much detail as you like). By faith I let go of each of these worries for today. I relinquish each of these situations to you, and ask you to give me that peace which passes understanding. And in the midst of this busy day, please give me a thankful heart.

ONE HUNDRED TEN

— ❧ —

Don't Toot My Own Horn

*Let another praise you, and not your own mouth; someone else,
and not your own lips.*

PROVERBS 27:2

Many years ago, there was a woman who reported to me who
was a truly excellent worker. She did her job about as well as
you could do it; she was honest and hard-working; she was
dependable and thorough; she was enthusiastic and energized.
But she was also a braggart.

Every opportunity she had, she would let you know what a
good job she did. She often told her co-workers how they
could improve if they did it her way. Nobody could refute her
work effort, but she sure turned people off with her bragging.
And because she talked about her achievements so much, I
was less inclined, as her manager, to recognize her in a formal
way because I knew all of my other employees were sick and
tired of hearing how good she was.

Wise Solomon gave us some good advice when he told us
to let others do the praising. I realize that too often people
don't get the praise they deserve, but it won't help matters to
start praising yourself. You can document your efforts and
achievements; you certainly don't have to cover them up. But
if you tend to talk too much about yourself and what you've
accomplished, you may turn some people off and damage
some relationships.

So when you're tempted to talk about your successes or achievements, why don't you wait and let another praise you? That's God's way.

Today's Challenge

To resist all temptations to toot my own horn.

Today's Prayer

Lord, please help me not to talk about myself or my achievements today. Make me mindful that it comes across as boasting and that it is not a good testimony. Also remind me that anything good I ever do is a gift from you, and that all credit should go to you.

ONE HUNDRED ELEVEN

—❦—

Trusting God for Children's Welfare

All your sons will be taught by the Lord, and great will be your children's peace.

ISAIAH 54:13

If you are a single working mom, my guess is that one of your persistent, gnawing fears is that your children will be adversely affected because of your situation. Maybe you've bought into the idea that you can't be a really good mother because you're single and you have to work. If you're a married working mom, you, too, probably spend sleepless nights wondering how your kids are going to turn out, since you aren't with them as much as you'd like to be.

Did you know that the Lord can teach your children in many ways, with and without you? It's hard for us moms to believe, but it's true that we are not the sole influence on our children, nor are we solely responsible for their maturity. God can teach your children in ways you've never imagined.

I look back on my years as a single mom, when my daughter was at home, and realize that many of those years were times when I was walking far off from the Lord. But even then, God taught my daughter, and in fact she relates that one of the strongest influences on her life was watching God work in *my* life.

Don't underestimate God's ability to teach your children and help them grow into mature young people. Claim this promise for your children; pray it daily into their lives. Trust a trustworthy God that great will be the peace of your children.

Today's Challenge

To learn to trust God for the welfare of my children, even when I'm not able to do everything for them that I want to do.

Today's Prayer

Lord, I ask you to teach my children today. Teach them the joy of walking with you; the discipline of an ordered life; how to relate to other people. Teach them all they need to know to be like Jesus. I claim your promise that they will be taught of the Lord and great will be their peace.

ONE HUNDRED TWELVE

— ❧ —

Evergreen Christian

Blessed is the man who trusts in the Lord, whose confidence is in him. He will be like a tree planted by the water that sends out its roots by the stream. It does not fear when heat comes; its leaves are always green. It has no worries in a year of drought and never fails to bear fruit.

JEREMIAH 17:7-8

If you live in the north, you develop a real love for evergreen trees. In the midst of winter when everything else is bare and brown, that evergreen tree is still tall and green, giving color and life to the otherwise bleak winter scene.

I really want to be an evergreen Christian, don't you? I want to be like the tree with roots so firmly entrenched that nothing turns its leaves brown or keeps it from bearing fruit. I want to learn to trust God so completely that whatever comes my way, I will have absolutely no fear!

Of course, a tree like this doesn't grow overnight. It takes time to get those roots down deep into that water supply. If I'm ever going to be an evergreen Christian, it will take time and discipline to get my roots firmly entrenched in God's water supply. I want each day to find me digging in deeper, pushing my roots of trust down further into Jesus. I want to trust the Lord more each day so that I can be ever green and ever fruitful.

Are you in a situation that seems rather dry, cold, or barren?

Perhaps you're facing some unknowns. As you go through this experience, you have two choices: to worry and fear, and thereby shrivel up and get dry and brown, or to trust God and push your roots deeper and deeper into that spring of living water, Jesus Christ. The only thing that makes sense is to trust God.

Today's Challenge

To be an evergreen Christian, one that bears fruit and stays green regardless of the circumstances.

Today's Prayer

Lord, I want to be like an evergreen tree, always fruitful for you. Help me to dig my roots down deeper every day. Show me where my roots are shallow and guide me into a deeper walk with you.

— ∾ —

Positive Attitude

But may the righteous be glad and rejoice before God; may they be happy and joyful.

PSALM 68:3

Could you honestly describe yourself as a happy and joyful person? If so, then you would have to be a positive person as well, right?

If we're going to be positive people, then we're going to have to fight the things that tend to bring us into negative territory. What are those things that can ruin your whole attitude?

Irritating managers? Lazy co-workers? Most of us have some of those people in our life. Impossible deadlines? Unrealistic expectations? These certainly can bring you into negative territory. Drab or drafty work space? Too much noise or confusion in your work area? Whatever these things are that tend to make you negative rather than positive, you need to identify them. Then, ask yourself three questions:

1. *Can I change this situation?* I find that most people gripe and complain, without making the first effort to find a solution. You have no grounds for complaint unless you've at least tried to find a solution.

2. *Is there some way I can compensate for this situation?* For example, if you have a dreary office, how can you perk it up? Maybe plants and posters will help.

3. Do I need to learn to live with this situation? Every job, every industry, every profession has certain negative aspects that simply go with the territory, and those you must learn to accept without allowing them to bring you down.

Think about the things that make you negative, and ask God to give you the grace and wisdom to rise above them and be the positive person you need to be for his glory.

Today's Challenge

To face the things that make me a negative person, and develop a plan to achieve victory over these things.

Today's Prayer

Lord, it's easy for me to slip into negative territory at times. I have special difficulty with _____. Please help me today by your power to be a joyful and happy person because of you and to be a more positive person than I normally am.

— ∿ —

Hope Helps

May the God of hope fill you with all joy and peace as you trust in him, so that you may overflow with hope by the power of the Holy Spirit.

ROMANS 15:13

I remember seeing a bumper sticker that read, "Since I've given up hope, I feel much better." This might be true for those who don't know God, but as Christians we can agree with the psalmist, who wrote: "My soul faints with longing for your salvation, but I have put my hope in your word" (Ps 119:81).

Christians never have to contemplate a life without hope, for our God is a God of hope. God not only brings us hope, he causes us to overflow with it.

Hope is the basis of faith, for Hebrews 11 says that faith is being sure of what we hope for. I have hope that I will spend eternity in heaven with God, and I will see Jesus face to face, as well as all my loved ones who also know Christ. That hope is absolutely vital to me, and my faith in Christ assures me that my hope is not wasted.

Romans 12:12 tells me that hope makes me joyful. Hope brings meaning into otherwise meaningless experiences. Hope helps me cope with all the things that happen that I just can't understand. Hope brings me joy.

In 1 Corinthians 13 I find that love always hopes. When we

truly love as we should, we will have great hope. We can hope for our loved ones, even when it looks hopeless.

No, I wouldn't want that bumper sticker on my car. Hope is a vital part of my life, and God is the only one who can truly give hope, through Jesus Christ our Lord. Here's a more appropriate bumper sticker: "But as for me, I will always have hope; I will praise you more and more" (Ps 71:14).

Today's Challenge
To rejoice in the hope that God has given me. Hope of heaven, hope of life with Jesus, hope of everything working out for good in my life.

Today's Prayer
Lord, thank you that you are a God of hope. My life is not hopeless, but rather it is filled with hope because of Jesus.

Is Jesus on Board?

When evening came, his disciples went down to the lake, where they got into a boat and set off across the lake for Capernaum. By now it was dark, and Jesus had not yet joined them.

JOHN 6:16-17

I always wonder why the disciples just went off and left Jesus. We read in verse 22 that they took the only boat. Did they forget Jesus? Surely not. Had they set a time to leave and Jesus was a no-show? Perhaps. Were they just tired of waiting for him to break away from the crowd? No, for Jesus had withdrawn to a mountain by himself to pray.

Of course, without Jesus on board the disciples were soon in trouble. The waters were rough. But Jesus walked out to them, in spite of the troubled waters—on top of the troubled waters!—and miraculously they were suddenly safe on the shore.

I wonder how often I leave without Jesus on board. Without waiting for him, without entrusting the journey to his care, doing everything by my own strength. And then the waters get rough and I realize Jesus is not on board. I have left without him.

We need to ask the Lord to teach us this simple lesson of not going ahead of him, of not trying to tackle our days without him. We need to start each journey—each day—with him on board. We never know what our waters will hold for us.

They may look quiet and calm when we start out, but storms can arise quickly, and we'll need Jesus when they do.

Undoubtedly the disciples didn't expect any difficulty. After all, they had crossed that lake on their own many times. Perhaps they even planned to come back later and get Jesus. But they soon discovered that they needed Jesus on board at all times.

So do I. So do you. Don't lift anchor until you've waited for him to join you. Spend quiet time with him each day before you set sail. You'll be so glad when you hit those troubled waters that you didn't leave home without him.

Today's Challenge

To be dependent upon Jesus every minute of my day and not try to tackle my day in my own strength.

Today's Prayer

Lord, I want you on board with me all day today. I invite you not only to be with me, but to pilot my boat and be in charge of my day. Help me not to lose sight of you all day long.

ONE HUNDRED SIXTEEN

— ✎ —

Laughing at the Days to Come

She is clothed with strength and dignity; she can laugh at the days to come.

PROVERBS 31:25

What does it mean to be able to laugh at the days to come? For me, it means that as I look at my personal future, I know that regardless of what happens to me, my future is secure. I've got eternal life right now because I've accepted Jesus as my Savior. So, regardless of what the future holds for me, I can laugh at the days to come.

It means that I can face an uncertain financial future, and laugh at it. I can't be certain that I'll have an income next week or next month or next year. But because my safety net is Jesus Christ, and not an income or a bank account, I can laugh at that prospect and say, "Never fear! God has promised to supply all my needs!"

As I look at the trouble all over the world and see how tenuous each of those situations is, I realize that it would only take a small spark to put us on the brink of another awful war. And while that certainly isn't a laughing matter, I can laugh at the fear and the oppression of those thoughts, because my God is sovereign, and nothing is going to happen in this world without his purpose being served.

You may be facing uncertainties and you may not know what the future will bring. But if your trust is in God—not in people, not in money, not in possessions or position—then you can laugh at the days ahead.

Ask God to show you how. It will bring the sweet relief and peace you've been looking for, as you learn to laugh at the days ahead. Those days are in God's hands, and he is perfectly capable of taking you through whatever will be.

Today's Challenge

To replace my fear of the future with the assurance that God is in control and I can truly laugh at the days ahead.

Today's Prayer

Lord, please help me to remember that you are sovereign and you are in control of me and my world. Please help me to overcome my fears of the days to come, and instead, because of faith in you, to laugh at the days to come.

ONE HUNDRED SEVENTEEN

— ❧ —

Learning to Relearn

I will remember the deeds of the Lord; yes, I will remember your miracles of long ago.

PSALM 77:11

As I start to prepare material for my radio program or messages for my speaking engagements, I often think, "I don't have anything new to say." And I start to panic because I haven't got a new idea or a new topic to present. But God reminds me that repetition is the way we learn.

Do you, like me, have to learn and relearn and relearn the lessons God wants to teach you? I'm amazed at the patience of our Lord, for I can be so slow to truly learn and obey all that I know. God will work on one area of my life, and I'll think we've made some progress. Then I'll look back a few weeks or months later and realize that I need to relearn what God has already taught me. How easily I forget; how easily I slip back into old habits and wrong ways of thinking.

What I'm learning from all this is that I must be prepared to relearn many times the things I've already learned. I think of the verse to the old hymn that says, "Prone to wander, Lord I feel it; prone to leave the God I love." Truly, "prone to wander" is a good description of me.

Let me encourage you today, if you find yourself in this same dilemma, learn to relearn. Go back and listen again to what God has already taught you. If there were books that spoke to your heart, read them again. If there were tapes that made an impact on you, get them out and listen again and again. Repeat and repeat what you already know.

In the Bible God was constantly urging his people to remember, to recite, to relearn what they had been dramatically taught already, because he knew that we are all prone to wander.

Today's Challenge

To continue to learn and relearn the important truths of God, and never to take for granted my walk with the Lord.

Today's Prayer

Lord, please deliver me from any kind of arrogance that would tempt me to think I've got any spiritual lesson learned. Help me to remember the things I've already learned, so that I do not lose what you have taught me.

— ᘓ —

Check Up on Your Book Cover

For we are taking pains to do what is right, not only in the eyes of the Lord but also in the eyes of men.

2 CORINTHIANS 8:21

This is the ninth book I've written, and each time the publisher retains control of the book's title and cover. That's because covers sell books, they tell me, so they want to be sure the cover and title are right. People do judge books by their covers.

Did you ever realize that people are judging you by your cover? Perception becomes reality, so how others perceive you, based on your external appearance, tends to influence greatly their opinion of you. I wish people didn't do that; but they do—and so do you and I. We all judge books by their covers.

The Apostle Paul reminds us that we should "take pains" to do what is right in the eyes of men. That doesn't mean that we should try to jump through everyone's hoops. But it does mean that we should do what we can to make a good first impression and present ourselves in the most favorable light possible.

Our covers are composed of style of dress, posture, eye contact, handshakes, smiles, tone of voice, word choices … a myriad of little things that add up to our "book cover." It will take some effort on our part to face our need to improve and then to do the things that will help us make a better impression. But, especially as ambassadors for Jesus Christ, we should do whatever we can to create a perception that is favorable.

Today's Challenge

To make an assessment of my personal "book cover" and determine areas that need some sprucing up.

Today's Prayer

Lord, please help me to see and hear myself the way others see and hear me so that I can more accurately assess areas where I need to improve. I want to do whatever I can do to be the best possible representative of you. Give me the desire and power to make these needed changes.

— ❧ —

Practice Joy

Be joyful always.

1 THESSALONIANS 5:16

That's the whole verse—three little words: "Be joyful always." Surely the apostle Paul was using hyperbole when he wrote this sentence. Could he have meant for us to take it seriously? Be joyful always?! Who ever heard of such a thing?

This is one of those "mission impossible" statements in the Bible that takes your breath away if you ever seriously consider it. And yet, God never asks us to do what he is not ready to equip us to do. He gives the orders and then supplies the power to obey! You and I *can* take it seriously; it *is* possible to have a joyful attitude at all times, by God's grace.

We hear a lot about attitude these days. Did you ever realize that your attitude is your choice? It's true. Nobody can force us to have a rotten attitude, no matter how rotten things are, if we don't want to. Of course, nobody can force us to have a good attitude, even on a good day, if we don't want to.

Have you slid into negative territory too often the past few days? You can solve your attitude problem on any day as you choose to "be joyful always."

How do you do that? By pushing out the negative thoughts with positive ones. By speaking words that encourage rather than words of doom and gloom. By reciting what you have to be thankful for, even when you don't feel thankful. By keeping this verse in front of your eyes as much as possible to remind you to "be joyful always." Remember, your attitude today is your choice.

Today's Challenge

To learn the secret of how to put into practice these three words: "Be joyful always."

Today's Prayer

Lord, today I will be working in an environment that is not always conducive to joy. Help me through your power to truly count my blessings and keep a joyful attitude throughout the day, no matter what is going on around me.

ONE HUNDRED TWENTY

— ✺ —

Fair-Weather Faith

Though the fig tree does not bud and there are no grapes on the vines, though the olive crop fails and the fields produce no food, though there are no sheep in the pen and no cattle in the stalls, yet I will rejoice in the Lord, I will be joyful in God my Savior.

HABAKKUK 3:17-18

I see a lot of fair-weather faith all around me—I see far too much in my own life at times. Faith-weather faith is the kind that is strong when things are going well, but when bad times hit, it falls apart.

It's not too difficult to have great faith when things are going well. Certainly we should be filled with praise and joy for all God's goodness to us. The psalmist expressed this kind of praise very well: "The Lord has done great things for us, and we are filled with joy" (Ps 126:3).

But what about those times when nothing good is happening? A mature Christian is one who praises even when there's no silver lining, no light at the end of the tunnel. Habakkuk said, even though things are just awful, yet I will rejoice in the Lord. I will be joyful in God my Savior. It's that orientation of our will that makes the difference. We make a choice to praise God and rejoice in him, regardless.

Where are you today? Good times in your life? Nice circumstances? Sometimes we forget to praise God for the good times and start to take things for granted. So, if things are going well, praise God and promise him that when the hard times hit, you'll praise him then, too.

Maybe it's not so good for you right now. Maybe you face tough days, heartaches, failures, and disappointments. Praise him anyway. When God sees that kind of faith and that setting of your will, he is pleased for he knows that your faith is not the fair-weather type. May that be true of each of us today.

Today's Challenge

To praise God, whether the day is a good one or a bad one.

Today's Prayer

Lord, even if everything goes wrong today, help me to rejoice in you anyway. And if today is pleasant and peaceful, may I never fail to give you praise for that as well. Help me not to be a fair-weather Christian.

— ∾ —

Jesus' Family

"Who are my mother and my brothers?" Then he [Jesus] looked at those seated in a circle around him and said, "Here are my mother and my brothers! Whoever does God's will is my brother and sister and mother."

MARK 3:33-35

I know that many people come from what we now call dysfunctional families. While I'm thankful that I have not personally had to deal with this, I know that it is very difficult to recover from a dysfunctional relationship with your parents or siblings. It seems to leave deep and permanent scars that often are very painful.

Notice what Jesus said about families; these words are found in three of the four gospels. How comforting this should be to those who have a dysfunctional family! When he was told that his mother and brothers were waiting outside to speak with him, Jesus declared that he had a much wider, more inclusive family than just his mother and brothers—that is, those who do God's will.

Isn't that something? You have a ready-made family if you're doing the will of God. If you feel the need for family—brothers, sisters, even children—Jesus can fill in that missing piece for you. He offers you himself, and he offers you his body, the church.

Notice that Jesus didn't say he'd be your father; that's

reserved for our heavenly Father; we are allowed as children of God to call God, "Abba Father," or dearest Father. But Jesus can be to you all of the other family roles, provided you meet the requirements: you must do the will of his Father.

This is a truth we can all rejoice in, but especially those who are struggling with broken or incomplete families here on earth. If your earthly family has some missing players, remember what Jesus said: *Whoever does God's will is my brother and sister and mother.*

Today's Challenge

To have a new understanding of how Jesus meets all my needs, even for the family I thought I'd never have.

Today's Prayer

Lord, thank you that you are to me all the missing pieces of my life. And thank you that I am a part of your family, and that my heavenly family is whole and healthy, without any of the dysfunctions of a human family.

ONE HUNDRED TWENTY-TWO

— ∼ —

Appreciate the Way God Made You

I praise you because I am fearfully and wonderfully made;
your works are wonderful.

PSALM 139:14

You are wonderful because you are a work of God, and all God's works are wonderful. God fashioned you in your mother's womb, and he knew you before you were born; your days were planned for you before any of them ever were. We can be secure and content in who we are, because God's hands made and formed us, and God doesn't make mistakes.

There is wonderful freedom in accepting who we are. Freedom from having to live up to others' expectations—or even our own. Freedom from having to be like others or compete with others. Freedom from the need to prove to the world that we are someone special, because we already know we're special to God. It really takes the monkey off our backs!

When you are not happy with who you are, you inflict great suffering on yourself. It causes you to be envious of others, to resent the success of others, to fight to get ahead of others, to be dependent upon the approval of others. All kinds of problems arise when you cannot accept and appreciate who you are.

Have you come to that place yet where you can truly say, "I like the way God has created me"? Oh, I hope so. It is not being proud to appreciate God's handiwork in you. Rather it brings glory to God, just as when you appreciate a work of art you bring honor to the artist.

Today's Challenge

To appreciate the way God has created me, knowing that all his works are wonderful.

Today's Prayer

Lord, thank you for your creativity in me. You created me from the inside out, knitting me together in my mother's womb, and I praise you that I am fearfully and wonderfully made. Forgive me for the times I've been so dissatisfied with the way you made me. Please keep me from comparing myself with others, and help me learn that when I appreciate your works, I also appreciate myself.

ONE HUNDRED TWENTY-THREE

— ∾ —

Work Reveals Your Character

The heavens declare the glory of God; the skies proclaim the work of his hands. Day after day they pour forth speech; night after night they display knowledge.

PSALM 19:1-2

Did you ever realize that your work tells what kind of person you are? The Bible tells us that the works of God reveal to us what kind of God he is. The beauty of his creation, the majesty and grandeur of his universe give us a clear view of his character and his personality.

That's true of us, as well. Now that's a little scary, when you think about it. Just suppose that someone who didn't know you at all was asked to write a description of you based upon an audit and inspection of your work. What would that audit reveal?

Are you careful to do your work thoroughly, or would your work reveal a careless attitude? Does your work show that you are considerate of the person at the receiving end or at the next stage of your work? Or would the inspector conclude that you're in a hurry to get through and get going, because your work is sloppy?

When your work involves dealing with other people, would it reveal an attitude of respect and concern for others? Do you think the inspector would conclude that you care about other people? Or would it reveal that you are callous toward other people, that you can't be bothered to be kind and considerate?

As I look at the work of God's hands, I know so much about his loving, caring nature. I see all around me evidence that he is a merciful and bountiful God, a God who wants to bestow blessings and goodness on me. His work reveals his character to me.

Our work reveals our character as well. At the end of each day we need to ask ourselves what kind of impression our work has left behind us. Think about the week that is just behind you. Would you be pleased to have someone describe you based on the work you've done this last week? It's a question we need to ask ourselves frequently.

Today's Challenge

To do my everyday work in such a manner that it exemplifies the character of Jesus Christ.

Today's Prayer

Lord, help me to remember all day long that how I do my work does indeed matter to you, and speaks volumes to those around me. May my work be pleasing in your sight today, O Lord.

— ❧ —

Are You a Has-Been?

As she [Phinehas' wife] was dying, the women attending her said, "Don't despair; you have given birth to a son." But she did not respond or pay any attention. She named the boy Ichabod, saying, "The glory has departed from Israel"— because of the capture of the ark of God and the deaths of her father-in-law and her husband.

1 SAMUEL 4:20-21

How would you like to be named Ichabod? It's not a lovely name, but what it means is even worse. Ichabod means "the glory is departed." In our vernacular today, we might say, "Are you a has-been?" Could it ever be said of me that the glory God has given to me through Jesus Christ is no longer present in my life?

When Phinehas' wife named her son Ichabod, it was because of the sin of Israel. They had disobeyed the Lord and the ark of God had been captured. The ark was where God met them, where they talked to him, where they received guidance. Their enemies had captured it because of Israel's sin and disobedience.

We can be spiritual "has-beens" when our lives are full of disobedience. I can think of so many Christians I know who were at one time mightily used by God. It could be said of them that they "have been" this or that for God, but because of their sin and disobedience, the glory has departed.

"Ichabod" is now their name.

In Christ we are given the right to be called the sons of God. That is glorious. We become the righteousness of Christ and are partakers of his holiness. That's really incredible. And yet, we can lose the glory of all that we have received from God if our lives are not continually in close contact with the Lord.

It takes a daily commitment, a disciplined life of time in God's Word, an absolute decision of our will to obey God and live by his principles, regardless. Without those elements in our everyday life, we can expect the glory to depart.

Today's Challenge

To search my heart and determine if some of God's glory has departed from my life because of sin or disobedience.

Today's Prayer

Lord, I don't want to be a "has-been," an "Ichabod." Please reveal to me any areas in my life where your glory has been dimmed or killed by my lack of love or zeal or obedience. I want to be restored to that original glory you gave me in Jesus Christ.

— ❧ —

Are You Tired?

Even youths grow tired and weary, and young men stumble and fall.

ISAIAH 40:30

Jesus was often tired while he was here on earth. You remember when he went to sleep on the boat and a terrible storm didn't awaken him? He was tired. We read in John 4 that he was tired from a long journey. I think there is abundant evidence that he frequently grew weary of dealing with people. You can hear the exhaustion in his voice when he says, "O unbelieving and perverse generation, how long shall I stay with you? How long shall I put up with you?" (Mt 17:17).

We can know that Jesus understands our tired bodies and minds, because he experienced all of that while he took the form of man here on earth. He sympathizes with our weaknesses and the limitations we face. Just knowing that helps me a lot.

Do you remember how exhausted Elijah was after his victorious encounter with Baal, where he performed mighty miracles of God and defeated the enemies? He was so tired, he wanted to die. You should expect to be weary after a spiritual high. Maybe God has been using you in an unusual way, and you've seen God's blessings in your life. Remember after those times to expect to feel weary.

So, it's OK to be tired. But we have to determine if we're

tired for the wrong reasons. Have you been trying to be all things to all people lately? That's exhausting—and you can never succeed. Perhaps you've taken on jobs God never intended you to do, and you're tired from trying to do too much. Maybe you're trying to do everything to total perfection. Perfectionists are usually very tired people.

You may be tired because you've got your priorities confused. There's always time to do God's will, but when we try to do more than God has given us to do, then we get into exhaustion and burnout.

Today's Challenge

To examine why I am tired and ask myself if it's normal, to-be-expected tiredness that will go away with some needed rest, or if it's because I have my priorities confused.

Today's Prayer

Lord, I know that you understand tired bodies, and I know that sometimes being tired is inevitable and necessary. But please help me to avoid doing things that create unnecessary fatigue and keep me exhausted. Help me to see where my priorities are misplaced.

ONE HUNDRED TWENTY-SIX

— ❧ —

Encourage the Timid

And we urge you, brothers, warn those who are idle, encourage the timid, help the weak, be patient with everyone.

1 THESSALONIANS 5:14

Do you know someone who has a timid personality? If you have never had a problem with timidity, it may be difficult to understand how painful shyness can be. Imagine what it would be like if every contact with someone you didn't know well made your heart beat faster, caused you to be self-conscious, and actually made you feel sick to your stomach. That is indeed the experience of many timid people.

How can we encourage the timid? Well, first, be sensitive to them. Many look perfectly confident, as they've learned to put on a good front. They appear to be loners, and many times people leave them alone because they think they want to be alone. In fact, they may even claim that they prefer to be alone. But often, deep inside, they are longing for someone who will be persistent enough to get to know them. So, we can encourage those who are timid by watching out for them, learning to include them, trying to make them comfortable in our presence.

Extreme timidity and shyness may be an outward sign of a lack of understanding of who you are in Christ and how God feels about you. Timid people often feel unworthy. So we can encourage them by helping them to understand that they are very worthwhile, especially if they are fellow believers.

If you're a shy or timid person, I want to encourage you. You're every bit as important to God as anyone else; he has made you special and unique. You have good things to offer the people in your life, and you need to be freed from your timidity so you can reach out to others, in your quiet way, and encourage them.

It's good we have some quiet people around to balance the rest of us. You don't have to become an extrovert in order to overcome shyness. But don't let your shyness or timidity keep you from enjoying who you are in Christ.

Today's Challenge

To become sensitive to those who are shy and timid and to reach out with encouragement, including them in my circle of friends.

Today's Prayer

Lord, in my busy day I often overlook people who are not loud or assertive. Help me today to notice the shy people, those who find it painful to interact in a group. Show me how to encourage those people today.

Grading on the Curve

But the plans of the Lord stand firm forever, the purposes of his heart through all generations.

PSALM 33:11

When I was a student there were many times I was thankful for professors who graded on the curve, so that my performance was compared with that of the entire class, rather than an absolute standard of perfection. In that way, what might have been a "C" paper became a "B."

What's important for us to remember, however, is that God never grades on the curve. In our society, values are often perceived to be adaptable or changeable, depending on the circumstances. And we sometimes get the mistaken idea that God operates like this, too, but it's just not true. God has put in place his unchanging absolutes. He doesn't make allowances based on our excuses or circumstances.

We can't go to God and say, "Lord, I know you've said sexual impurity is a sin, but I'm sure you'll make an exception in my case. After all, I really love this person." Or "God, I know I lied about that, but you know that it was necessary in order to please my boss. So, please excuse me from your principle about telling the truth." Or "I know I'm supposed to be loving and kind, but I'm sure you weren't talking about people like my co-worker, so please make an allowance for me in this case." God's principles are absolute. We cannot bargain with him.

The Bible says, "Let God be true and every man a liar." That means if every person on earth disagrees with God's standards, it will never change his principles. God doesn't worry about popularity contests or the latest polls. He is God and we are his creation. He is not trying to please or impress us.

So be careful that you don't allow this world system to cause you to think that God will grade you on the curve. Remember that his principles are absolute and it is our responsibility to know them and obey them. It truly is that simple.

Today's Challenge

To make certain I don't lower my own standards of integrity to conform to the world's shifting principles.

Today's Prayer

Lord, show me where I have been deceived into lowering my own standards in conformity with the world system, and give me the grace and power to stand firm on your Word and never compromise the principles of Scripture in my life.

— ∼ —

Our Extravagant God

Your love, O Lord, reaches to the heavens, your faithfulness to the skies. Your righteousness is like the mighty mountains, your justice like the great deep.

PSALM 36:5-6

Extravagance is generally considered an undesirable trait. It's defined as excessive, wasteful, exorbitant. Yet, when I look at God, I see extravagance as one of his attributes. Consider how excessive God is in his dealings with us.

His mercy keeps us from having to pay the due penalty for our sins. The Bible tells us his mercies are new every day, and they last forever. So, he is just piling up mercy upon mercy each day, extravagant mercy, given to us free of charge.

Then there's his grace, which goes beyond mercy to give us undeserved blessings, and we know that he makes all grace abound to us in all things at all times, giving us all we need, so that we will abound in every good work (see 2 Cor 9:8). Abundant, rich, extravagant grace.

As for God's forgiveness, he goes beyond forgiving us and separates our sins from us as far as the east is from the west, then proceeds to forget every blemish and stain. Can you forgive and forget? That's God's kind of forgiveness—excessive, extravagant.

Not only do we have a God who allows us to come to him, we have a God who seeks us. Can you imagine that? Not only are we allowed to worship him, we can call him Abba Father and come boldly to his throne. Not only can we accept him as our Savior, but he comes to abide in us. The abundance of God's love toward us is beyond our comprehension.

When we consider God's extravagance toward us, can we continue to respond to him in meager ways, doing as little as possible, grudgingly giving our time and money, relinquishing only parts of ourselves, holding back on God? Do something extravagant for God today!

Today's Challenge

To be more aware of God's extravagant gifts to me and to be willing to be more extravagant in what I do for him.

Today's Prayer

Lord, I'm often so stingy with what I give to you and others. I seem to be overly concerned that I might give more than I have to. Please give me a heart that is so full of your extravagant love for me that I am willing to be extravagant in what I do for you and others.

ONE HUNDRED TWENTY-NINE

— ∾ —

Faith Before Miracles

And he [Jesus] did not do many miracles there [in his hometown] because of their lack of faith.

MATTHEW 13:58

As I was reading this passage, I thought, "Why didn't Jesus perform miracles so that they would have faith in him? The miracles would have produced faith." But then I remembered the many times he refused to do miracles in order to produce faith in people.

Faith is not produced by miracles; miracles are a result of faith. Jesus never jumps through hoops for us to try to convince us to have faith in him. After all, Jesus doesn't need our validation of who he is, and it is sinful arrogance to think that God must prove himself to us. We must come to God by faith if we come at all, and faith is the evidence of things hoped for, being certain of what we do not see. Therefore, miracles don't produce faith. They strengthen our faith, but the faith must come before the miracles.

As a matter of fact, I think if Jesus had tried to produce faith through miracles, he never could have done enough. He would have had to come up with bigger and better miracles all the time, because we humans become jaded rather easily, and the miracle that produced faith one day would be commonplace the next. So Jesus, who understands human nature better than anyone else, knows that miracles and signs do not produce faith.

If you haven't seen many miracles in your life lately, it might be because Jesus doesn't see much faith there. Do you have reservations about your faith in Christ because you haven't seen the miracles you want? If so, you've got the cart before the horse. God is looking for faith, which by definition means you don't have the miracle yet, and then his power will be released on your behalf.

Today's Challenge

To please God by trusting him and having faith in him regardless of what's happening around me. Not to ask God for a miracle of some sort in order for me to have faith in him.

Today's Prayer

Lord, I want to affirm to you that I trust you, for you are a trustworthy God and my faith is based on your Word and your faithfulness to me. Therefore, I do not ask for evidence before I trust. Rather, I trust you even when the evidence is hard for me to see. Lord, please help me to trust you more.

ONE HUNDRED THIRTY

— ∿ —

A Living Sacrifice

Therefore, I urge you, brothers, in view of God's mercy, to offer your bodies as living sacrifices, holy and pleasing to God— which is your spiritual worship.

ROMANS 12:1

This living sacrifice concept is one that can be rather baffling. Sacrifices don't sound too good to me to begin with, and certainly sacrificing my own body tends to make me a little nervous—how about you?

What did the apostle Paul mean to tell us in this verse? How can we present our bodies as living sacrifices? Well, the first good news we see is that it is to be a *living* sacrifice, so there's no physical death implied here; quite the opposite.

In Romans 6 Paul wrote that we are to offer the parts of our body to Christ as instruments of righteousness. So we can literally go through the parts of our bodies and relinquish each of them to his service for the day, like this:

"Lord, here are my feet. They are yours today. May I walk as you would walk, go where you want me to go. Here are my hands, Lord. I give them to you today so that what I do with them will bring honor to you. Here are my eyes, so that I can see as you see. Here are my ears; may I listen to what you would listen to. Lord, I give you my tongue today. I ask you to control all the words formed by my tongue, that they be words of help and healing. My brain is yours, Lord; I want to think your thoughts. Here's my heart, Lord. Put in my heart your love and compassion for all the people I will see today. I present my body to you as a sacrifice that will live for you today, Lord, not for me. I do this by faith and trust you for the reality."

Committing each part of your body daily to God as a sacrifice keeps fresh in your mind the importance of every area of your conduct. I find this makes a significant difference in my day. If you sincerely do this on a daily basis, you will discover that you will be less and less conformed to this world and more and more conformed to the image of Jesus Christ.

Today's Challenge

To take seriously this challenge to present every part of my body to God as a living sacrifice on a daily basis.

Today's Prayer

Lord, today I give you each part of my body (present every part of your body). I want to be a living sacrifice for you today.